PASS PMP IN 21 DAYS II – PRACTICE TESTS

Step 1I: Evaluate

KAVITA SHARMA

SIGNIFICANT CONTRIBUTOR – PMBOK 6TH EDITION

BASED ON THE NEW PMP CONTENT

VERSION: 7.1, RELEASED ON: 3 June 2022

I want to thank all my students for making this book possible and continue updating it. This is the 7th version of the book in your hands.

Your feedback emails/WhatsApp keep me motivated.

Thanks to all of you.

कर्मण्येवाधिकारस्ते मा फलेषु कदाचन ।
मा कर्मफलहेतुर्भुर्मा ते संगोऽस्त्वकर्मणि ॥

It is the work that you control and not the outcome.

TABLE OF CONTENTS

PREFACE

HI FROM KAVITA SHARMA

This book is written with the intent of covering as many topics as possible through questions. The answers will help you understand the concepts.

If you follow the questions and keywords – you will be able to arrive at the correct answers. That's what is needed to pass the PMP exam.

The PMP Exam tests your skills and understanding of the concepts. If you know them, You will pass.

The design principles of the book are:

→ Broad coverage of topics through questions
→ The answer should simplify the concept
→ Give more references to understand the concept, if any.

The book comprises of is questions from various domains as per current ECO, and it should be picked up after your 35 PDU course.

Set aside 2-4 hours each day. Do prescribed reading and assess yourself. One chapter one day. That's all. One step at a time.

You are at evaluate step. Step 2.

THE 21 DAYS TEST PREP PLAN

Phase	Day	Book Chapters	Commitment (Hours)
Phase: Understand and Evaluate			
	Day 1	1. Agile	2 - 4 Hours
	Day 2	2.1 People | Team	2 - 4 Hours
	Day 3	2.2 People | Stakeholders	
	Day 4	2.3 People | Communications	2 - 4 Hours
	Day 5	3.1 Business Environment	2 - 4 Hours
	Day 6	3.2 Business Environment | Integration	2 - 4 Hours
	Day 7	4.1 Process | Scope Management	2 - 4 Hours
	Day 8	4.2 Process | Schedule Management	2 - 4 Hours
	Day 9	4.3 Process | Cost Management	2 - 4 Hours
	Day 10	4.4 Process | Quality Management	2 - 4 Hours
	Day 11	4.5 Process | Risk Management	2 - 4 Hours
	Day 12	4.6 Process | Procurement Management	2 - 4 Hours
	Day 13	Buffer	2 - 4 Hours
	Day 14	Buffer	NA
Phase: Simulate			
	Day 15	Full-Length PMP Test	4-5 Hours
	Day 16	Full-Length PMP Test	4-5 Hours
	Day 17	Full-Length PMP Test	4-5 Hours
	Day 18	Full-Length PMP Test	4-5 Hours
	Day 19	Buffer - If you missed any day	NA
	Day 20	Buffer - If you missed any day	NA
	Day 21	**Pass the PMP EXAM**	

You can refer following documents for studies:

- Agile Practice Guide available ta PMI.org
- PMBOK 6th Edition available ta PMI.org
- Pass PMP in 21 Days I – Study Guide by Kavita Sharma

AGILE

1. AGILE

RECOMMENDED READINGS

Agile practice guide at PMI.org (Available for PMI members)
OR
Pass PMP in 21 Days I – Study Guide:
Chapter 3. Agile – Let's Get Started

1.1 AGILE QUESTIONS

1. Scrum, an agile practice, uses ceremonies that help in establishing the cadence of meetings and preparing the report of the project as it progresses. The agile ceremonies include Sprint Planning, Daily Stand-up, Sprint Review, and _____.

    A. Sprint Retrospective
    B. Sprint Iterations
    C. Scrum Retrospective
    D. Scrum Iterations

2. A letter I is written against my name in the team RACI chart. What is expected of me?

    A. I should be able to provide instructions to the team
    B. I should be informed of team communications.

3. You are working on the project resource calendar of your project. What can you find in project resource calendars? (Select 3)

    ☐ A. Team holidays
    ☐ B. Team members' availability
    ☐ C. Working time/days
    ☐ D. Milestones
    ☐ E. Resource skills

4. Jerry is developing the team charter for his team. He is writing the project vision, ground rules, and important milestones in the charter. Is this the correct content for the team charter?

    A. True
    B. False

5. You are part of an agile team working as a team member. Which event would you be part of? (Select all that apply)

    ☐ A. Sprint Planning
    ☐ B. Daily Scrum
    ☐ C. Sprint Review
    ☐ D. Sprint Retrospective
    ☐ E. Kick-off Meeting

6. Which 2 Scrum events are mandatory for Scrum Master to attend?

    ☐   A. Sprint Planning

    ☐   B. Daily Scrum

    ☐   C. Sprint Review

    ☐   D. Sprint Retrospective

    ☐   E. Kick-off Meeting

7. You are part of an agile team working as a Scrum Master. Which Scrum events are mandatory for you to attend? (Select all that apply)

    ☐   A. Sprint Planning

    ☐   B. Daily Scrum

    ☐   C. Sprint Review

    ☐   D. Sprint Retrospective

    ☐   E. Kick-off Meeting

8. At the end of every sprint, the team must complete a product increment that is potentially releasable.

    A.   True

    B.   False

9. An agile team can use the following artifacts to track the project progress (Select 2)

    ☐   A. Burndown Chart

    ☐   B. Burnup Chart

    ☐   C. Expected monetary value chart

    ☐   D. Daily stand-up

10. What is the recommended size of agile teams as per Scrum methodology?

    A.   5 to 9 members

    B.   6 to 9 members

    C.   5 to 10 members

    D.   4 to 11 members

11. The Product Owner asked the developers to add a very important item to a sprint that is in progress. What should be your response to it as a Project Manager?

    A.   Let's do this. Adapting to change is the reason we selected the agile methodology for our project.

    B.   Let's add this item to the Product Backlog and revisit it in the next iteration planning meeting.

12. The Product Backlog should be ordered by:

    A.   Value, least valuable items at the top and most valuable at the bottom

    B.   Size, small items are at the top, and large items are at the bottom.

    C.   Risk, safer items are at the top, and riskier items are at the bottom.

    D.   Value, most valuable items at the top and least valuable at the bottom.

13. Jerry explained the usage of the timebox for his project. He mentioned that using a 2-week timebox helped the team deliver value to the customer in incremental order. Which project life cycle is used by Jerry?

    A.   Predictive methodology

    B.   Agile methodology

    C.   Incremental methodology

    D.   Iterative methodology

14. You are an expert on agile and are coaching the current management and projects on agile practices. Since the project scope is huge and the urgency to deliver is high, two teams are working concurrently on the project. Both are following agile practices. What would be the most helpful tool for them to integrate the work as a whole?

    A.   Scrum of Scrum

    B.   Agile of Agile

    C.   Daily Meetings

    D.   Video Calls

15. Product roadmaps are used to

    A.   Provide vision to the Development Team

    B.   Provide data to monitor and control the project

16. The agile team should always focus on?

    A.   Delivering using Timeboxes

    B.   Estimating better to deliver user stories within Timebox

    C.   Using Kanban to improve quality

    D.   Delivering value by using prioritization methods

17. You are working with a solar panel manufacturer. The solar panel product goes through various stages before it can be deemed completed and ready to ship. Stage 1 can handle 10,000 solar panels per day; however, the last stage, i.e., storage and shipping, can store and ship only 8000 units per day. Which methodology would you recommend to handle such a scenario?

A.   Kanban pull system

B.   Kanban push system

C.   Agile pull system

D.   Agile push system

18.   **You are coaching the new agile team to work using the agile framework to deliver value. The team has started working on the iteration and found that some of the required software is not available to finish the selected Product Backlog item? What would be your suggestion to the team?**

A.   Refocus the iteration to achieve team's infrastructure instead of delivering an Increment.

B.   Declare to senior management that the Team is not ready for Scrum.

C.   Show it as an issue and work to complete the rest of the sprint backlog.

D.   Ask Product Owner to accept partially done Increments.

19.   **To build and deliver the defect-free increment for the next iteration, the Project Manager should focus on**

A.   Burndown charts for clear updates and delivery

B.   Retrospective meetings to improve team processes

C.   Sprint planning meetings to prioritize value

D.   The core values of agile for team harmony

20.   **How would you define Agile?**

A.   A methodology that accelerates collecting the requirements of the project early on in the project.

B.   A framework that is divided into people, process, and business environment

C.   A methodology to manage large and complex programs

D.   An iterative, time-boxed approach to delivering value to the business

21.   **The incremental project life cycle is one of the agile project life cycles.**

A.   True

B.   False

22.   **In the case of agile methodology, when does an iteration considered complete?**

A.   When the customer acceptance is over

B.   When the timebox is completed

C.   When the team finishes with all sprint backlog items

D.   When the Product Owner decides

23. **What are typical items discussed in the daily stand-up? (Select all that apply)**

    ☐   A. What did I do yesterday

    ☐   B. What is the plan for today

    ☐   C. How is my morale today

    ☐   D. Any issues hampering the progress

    ☐   E. Conflicts with other members, if any

24. **Which collaboration tools can facilitate team efficiency in a virtual environment? (Select 2)**

    ☐   A. Team task boards

    ☐   B. Your laptop

    ☐   C. Facebook connect

    ☐   D. Team Kanban board

25. **When many Development Teams are working on a single product, what describes the definition of "done?"**

    A.   Each Development Team defines and uses its own. The differences are discussed and reconciled during a Scrum of Scrum meeting.

    B.   Each Development Team uses its own but must make its definition clear to all other Teams, so the differences are known.

    C.   All Development Teams must have a definition of "done" that makes their combined work potentially releasable.

    D.   There should be one definition of "done" that should be followed by all the teams so that integration is smoother

26. **In the sprint planning meeting, the Product Backlog item should conform to _____ so that the team can consider it for upcoming iteration?**

    A.   The PBI should conform to the definition of done.

    B.   The PBI should conform to the definition of ready.

    C.   The PBI should conform to the readiness of done.

    D.   The PBI should conform to the definition of value.

27. **Define Sprint Review:**

    A.   It is a review of the team's activities during the Sprint.

    B.   It is the meeting where the Scrum Team and stakeholders inspect the outcome of the Sprint.

    C.   It is a demo at the end of the Sprint for everyone in the organization to provide feedback on the work done.

D.   It is the appraisal meeting of the Development Team

28.   Since the project required a faster outcome and more work, your agile coach made three teams of 8,9, and 6 people to perform the work in parallel. You all are using agile PLC to deliver work. Which 2 tools can help you collaborate across teams?

☐   A. Daily standups

☐   B. Scrum of Scrum meetings

☐   C. Scaled agile practices

☐   D. Scrum events

29.   When multiple teams work together, each team should maintain a separate Product Backlog.

A.   True

B.   False

30.   Which role in agile should know the most about the business objective, alternative, and release plans?

A.   Product Owner

B.   Project Manager

C.   Customer

D.   Scrum Master

31.   During the daily stand-up meeting, the Scrum Master's role is to:

A.   Lead the discussions

B.   Make sure required questions are asked

C.   Facilitate the meeting so that everyone gets to talk

D.   Coach and observe as a passive member

32.   While selecting the team members for my agile team, I should focus more on:

A.   Attitude. Skills do not matter - attitude matters

B.   Team members who have generic skills

C.   Team members who have competency in core skills (I shaped)

D.   Team members who have a broad level of skill plus specialty in-depth (T shaped)

33. **What are the typical roles in SCRUM methodology? (Select 3)**

    ☐ A. Product Owner

    ☐ B. Scrum Master

    ☐ C. Users

    ☐ D. Developers

    ☐ E. Testers

    ☐ F. Customer

    ☐ G Development Team

34. **Select the 3 Scrum artifacts:**

    ☐ A. Product Backlog

    ☐ B. Gantt chart

    ☐ C. Sprint backlog

    ☐ D. Burndown chart

    ☐ E. Communication plan

35. **An agile team is busy finishing the sprint. Meanwhile, you get a request from a stakeholder to share the project progress to date. What would you do? You are Scrum Master in the team.**

    A. Invite the stakeholder to the daily stand-up meeting

    B. Send him the last iteration review minutes

    C. Send him the project roadmap

    D. Invite the stakeholder to see the project burndown chart

36. **What is the primary role of a Product Owner?**

    A. Product Owner is a fancy name for the Project Manager in agile

    B. Product Owner is responsible for providing clarity on the product specifications

    C. Product Owner is a people manager in agile teams

    D. Product owner shows and cares for the team using servant leadership traits

37. **Which of the 2 ceremonies are executed after all sprint development and before starting the next one?**

    A. Sprint review and sprint retrospective

    B. Sprint review and sprint planning

    C. Daily stand-up and sprint review

    D. Sprint retrospective and sprint planning

38. Kanban board is an example of:

    A. Toyota production system

    B. Information refrigerator

    C. Information radiator

    D. High-tech and low-touch system

39. During a planning session, the Product Owner and the team sort the stories from the backlog into must-have, should-have, could-have, and won't-have. The must-haves top the chart, and a few should-haves get selected for implementation during the iteration. Which prioritization technique did the team follow?

    A. Kano model analysis

    B. Weighted prioritization technique

    C. Must-Have Prioritization Analysis

    D. MoSCoW technique

40. Which conflict resolution techniques result in a lose-lose outcome?

    A. Problem Solving

    B. Avoiding

    C. Compromising

    D. Forcing

41. Select the ODD one:

    A. Responding to change over following a plan.

    B. Customer collaboration over contract negotiation.

    C. Customer interactions over processes and tools.

    D. Working software over comprehensive documentation.

42. When you took a handover from the last Project Manager, you saw that the team was sitting in groups of 2 while one person was busy doing the work, and the other person was pinpointing mistakes or observing. This can be referred to as:

    A. Pair programming

    B. Invasion of privacy

    C. Agile methodology to work

    D. Kanban's way of working

43. Select the items which can be part of the definition of done (Total 4):

☐ A. Code is checked in the version control repository

☐ B. Time sheets are updated

☐ C. Peer review is done

☐ D. Naming guidelines for the code are followed

☐ E. Daily stand-ups are attended

☐ F. Status report is sent

☐ G Acceptance test cases are conducted and passed

44. Leaving low-priority requirements at a high level but sufficiently detailing the high priority (and immediate) ones are called _____.

A. Incremental development

B. Progressive elaboration

C. Version control

D. Continuous improvement

45. Team Alfa has a velocity of 25 story points, and Team Beta has a team velocity of 50 story points over a 2-week iteration. What does this mean?

A. Team Beta is more efficient

B. Team Beta has more capacity

C. Team Beta is more mature

D. Velocity of two teams cannot be compared

46. I and V and S in INVEST stands for _____,_____ , and _____

☐ A. Small

☐ B. Valuable

☐ C. Verifiable

☐ D. Interesting

☐ E. Independent

☐ F. Specific

47. How does value stream mapping helps in agile projects?

A. To visualize workflow to converse with the customer

B. To identify and eliminate waste from the process

C. Its a good activity to keep the team learning new skills

D. To keep the team busy and motivated

48. The Product Owner is looking at the Product Backlog, shuffling priorities, and adding details to the PBIs. And removing some that are no longer necessary. This activity is referred to as:

    A. Product refinement

    B. Backlog refinement

    C. Sprint grooming

    D. User story refinement

49. Which of the following represents the richest and most effective mode of communication in a virtual team?

    A. Recorded video messages

    B. Audio calls /meetings

    C. Video conferences/meetings

    D. Chats

50. What could be the best sequence of events while using an agile methodology (Drag and Drop question)

    A. Sprint review meeting

    B. Sprint planning meeting

    C. Sprint retrospective meeting

    D. Daily stand-up

51. Your team is using planning poker, and you are given some cards. What are the most likely values in the cards?

    A. T-shirt sizes S, M, L, XL, XXL, etc

    B. Random numbers as per your team's suggestions

    C. Odd number 1, 3, 5, 7, 9, 11, etc.

    D. Fibonacci series like 1, 2, 3, 5, 8, 13, 21, 34, etc

52. What are typical activities as a servant leader (Select 3)

    ☐ A. Coach team on team values and agile principles

    ☐ B. Make sure daily stand-ups happen and are conducted properly

    ☐ C. Come up with a detailed project plan at the end of the planning session

    ☐ D. Advocate the team's position to stakeholders

    ☐ E. Directs the team to follow agile principles

53. **Which conflict resolution techniques result in a win-lose outcome?**

   A.   Problem Solving

   B.   Forcing

   C.   Avoiding

   D.   Compromising

54. **Which of the following can help manage the virtual (distributed team)? (Select 3)**

   ☐   A. Rotations of the team members if travel budget permits.

   ☐   B. Sending emails regularly

   ☐   C. Kick-off meeting and minutes

   ☐   D. Planning a face time window for all members where possible

   ☐   E. Sensitivity and awareness of cultural diversity training to all members

55. **You are using the 100-point method to prioritize user stories in your team. How does it work?**

   A.   The team members are given a set of 100 stories to prioritize.

   B.   The team members are given 100 minutes to prioritize the user stories.

   C.   The team members are given 100 points that they can allocate to stories based on value as per their thought process

   D.   The team members are given 100 points that they can share among other team members to vote for the best user story

56. **A user story reads: "As a user of the product, I want to buy it online.". Is this user story correct and complete?**

   A.   True

   B.   False

57. **Which of the following is the best Agile team?**

   A.   An Agile team that collaborates and self-organizes continuously.

   B.   An Agile team that has no one to blame if things go wrong.

   C.   An Agile team with specialists.

   D.   An Agile team that avoids conflicts.

58. **Your team uses thumb voting to make decisions. One of your team members, while discussing a project item, showed the thumb sideways. What does it mean?**

   A.   The team member agrees with the decision

   B.   The team member is taking a neutral stand

   C.   The team member is in disagreement with the decision

   D.   The team member has shown strong support for the decision

59. At the end of the iteration, the team observes that they have completed only 50% of an initially estimated 12 story points. How many story points from this story would count toward the team's velocity?

   A.   Zero story point

   B.   12 story points

   C.   6 story points

   D.   50 story points

60. _____ is the minimum set of features that can be released to see the adoption by users for a product.

   A.   Minimum viable product

   B.   Maximum value product

   C.   Minimum features product

   D.   Maximum feature project

1.2 AGILE ANSWERS

Answer	Why
Answer 1 - A	Sprint Planning, Daily Stand-up, Sprint Review, and Sprint Retrospective are Agile ceremonies defined in Scrum.
Answer 2 - B	RACI, I should be informed of team communications. A responsibility assignment matrix, also known as the RACI matrix, can help in clarifying the team's roles. R stands for Responsible, A for accountable, C for consult, and I for Inform.
Answer 3 - A,B,C	The project team should be aware of and hence is part of the project calendar: • Team holidays • Team members availability • Working time/days Milestone is part of the schedule. Resource skills are part of the team training register or team details.
Answer 4 - FALSE	A team charter lists the team values, agreements, and operating guidelines and establishes clear expectations regarding acceptable behavior by project team members. Milestones are not part of the team charter. Having a working agreement for the team that articulates what the team values, how the team works together, and how they make decisions enables the team to have ground rules and aid in conflict resolution. The format and detail of a team charter can vary based on the expectations and culture of the team.
Answer 5 – A, B,C,D	An agile team member is expected to be part of all the sprint events. A kick-off meeting is not a recognized scrum/agile event.
Answer 6 – A, C	**Sprint Planning** Sprint planning involves the entire Scrum Team: the Development Team, Product Owner, and Scrum Master. **Daily Scrum** The mandatory participants at the Daily Scrum are the Development Team. The Scrum Master typically attends but is optional.

The Product Owner is invited but doesn't have to attend.

Sprint Review

The entire Scrum Team attends the sprint review.

Any stakeholders, senior managers, and other affected departments (e.g., marketing, customer support) are invited to participate and give feedback. Scrum teams should invite as many people as the room can hold--diverse feedback is essential for creating excellent products.

Sprint Retrospective

Sprint retrospectives are for the Scrum Team, which would include the Development Team, Scrum Master, and Product Owner. In practice, Product Owners are recommended but not mandatory attendees.

Kick-off meeting

This is not a planned scrum event.

7 - A, C, D	A Scrum Master should attend all the Scrum Events; however, daily meetings are driven by the Development Team, and other roles are optional.
8 - TRUE	That's TRUE. At the end of every sprint, the team must complete a product increment that is potentially releasable, meaning that meets their agreed-upon definition of done. The increment should be released or not - that's a decision for the Product Owner to take.
9 - TRUE	Sprint burndown/burnup charts help teams gauge whether they will complete the work of a sprint. EMV is typically used to assess risk and not progress. The daily standup is not a tool but an event.
10 - A	Most Agile and Scrum training courses refer to a 7 +/- 2 rule. That is, agile or Scrum teams should be 5 to 9 members
11 - B	The iterations are short and should not be disturbed. A good approach is that the value of the items should be discussed in the Iteration planning meeting.
12 - D	Typically - the Product Backlog is groomed along with the Development Team to bring clarity to the PBIs (Product Backlog items). The Product Backlog items should be clear and should be

	ready. Higher value items should be selected for iteration/sprint to produce value for the business.
13 - B	The timebox, i.e., producing deliverables in a predefined amount of time 1-4 weeks, is used in agile approaches. Don't be confused with iterative. The iterative methodology may not use the timebox approach. The agile approach is iterative and uses a timebox.
14 - A	Scrum of Scrum is a meeting to integrate the work and issues between the Scrum teams.
15 - A	Product Roadmaps are owned and developed by the Product Owner in consultation with the Development Team. The roadmap guides the team and acts as the vision for the product releases.
16 - D	Agile teams focus on delivering value to customers.
17 - A	In a Kanban pull system, a pull signal is triggered when the number of cards in a column drops beneath the specified limit. This signals to the previous column that a new task can move further. Once the work in progress limit is reached, no more tasks may be pulled until an outstanding one has been completed first.
18 - C	The Development Team should be enabled to carry out the tasks as per the sprint/iteration. Ensure that the team has all the requisite software/hardware to complete the timeboxed iteration. However, you cannot stop the work and let people sit ideal. So let the team finish the work to complete the Sprint Backlog.
19 - B	Sprint retrospectives can help identify the problem areas. This, in turn, can improve the overall environment and processes for team morale and team productivity.
20 - D	An iterative, time-boxed approach to deliver value to the business.
21 - FALSE	Agile is an iterative approach, i.e., the increments/sprints deliver value. Agile uses the timebox approach. Incremental project life cycles are adaptive project life cycles.
22 - B	A sprint/iteration in the agile projects is timeboxed. I.e., the iteration is over when the time finishes.
23 - A, B, D	The typical questions asked and answered in the daily meeting are: • Task completed before the meeting (Yesterday)

- Tasks Planned (Today)
- Issues/Risks

24 - A, D	Working together using a shared taskboard to check progress and collaboration would be a great addon. The laptop is the hardware to enable such collaboration.
25 - D	Having one single definition of done ensures that there are no gaps in understanding between teams.
26 - B	The PBI items should comply with DOR so that the team can estimate better and consider the items for the sprint. One of the DOR criteria can be INVEST criteria.
27 - B	The sprint review is the meeting where the Scrum Team and stakeholders **inspect** the outcome of the Sprint. The action points are needed to plan for the next iterations.
28 - B, C	Scrum of Scrum and scaled agile framework can be used in the case of bigger agile projects (scaled projects).
29 - FALSE	No. Having two Product Backlogs for one product will add to the confusion. Product Owner can have categories where the sub-Product Owner(if required) can work with each Development Team.
30 - A	The Product Owner is accountable for maximizing the value of the product resulting from the work of the Scrum Team. The Product Owner should have a vision, roadmap, and tentative release plans for the product to direct and guide the Development Team.
31 - D	The Scrum Master role is more of a servant leadership style. The scrum master is supposed to enable the team, not lead or direct.
32 - D	Yes, I agree with the first one where attitude comes first, but that's for all the time relevant for all teams while hiring. Since the iterations are timeboxed for agile teams, a T-skilled team can be more effective than I shaped.
33 - A,B,G	In Scrum, there are three roles: Product Owner, Development Team, and Scrum Master. Together these are known as the Scrum Team.
34 - A, C, D	Scrum artifacts are Product Backlog, Scrum Backlog, and Burndown chart.

35 - D	Instead of creating the report, ask the stakeholder to visit the team area or give access to the tracking tool for reports. Agile teams update the project progress daily. A burndown chart shows the team's progress and is updated daily.
36 - B	A Product Owner liaison with various departments is the KEY point of contact for the Development Team to clarify the product specifications (PBIs). He/she is involved in grooming the Product Backlog to ensure that the Product Backlog items are clear and provide value when developed and released.
37 - A	Sprint Review and Sprint Retrospective meetings are the two meetings that are held after the development is complete or the timebox is over. The Development Team showcases the outcome using the Sprint review meeting. A Sprint Retrospective provides insights into best practices and is one of the MUST ceremonies.
38 - C	"Information radiator" is the generic term for any of a number of handwritten, drawn, printed, or electronic displays that a team places in a highly visible location so that all team members, as well as passers-by, can see the latest information at a glance: count of automated tests, velocity, incident reports, etc.
39 - D	The MoSCoW method is a prioritization technique to reach a common understanding with stakeholders on the importance they place on the delivery of each requirement. The term MoSCoW itself is an acronym derived from the first letter of each of four prioritization categories: M - Must have S - Should have C - Could have W - Won't have
40 – C	Compromising is a lose-lose as both the parties feel that their opinions are not considered.
41 – C	The agile manifesto is: **Individuals and interactions over processes and tools** Working software over comprehensive documentation Customer collaboration over contract negotiation Responding to change over following a plan

	The option is written as "Customer interactions over processes and tools," but it should have been "Individuals and interactions over processes and tools."
42 – A	Pair programming is an agile software development technique in which two programmers work together at one workstation. One, the driver, writes code while the other, the observer or navigator, reviews each line of code as it is typed in. The two programmers switch roles frequently.
43 - A,C,D,G	The definition of done is an agreed-upon list of the activities necessary to get a product increment to a done state by the end of a sprint. A. Code is checked in the version control repository C. Peer review is done D. Naming guidelines for the code are followed G. Acceptance test cases are conducted and passed The definition of done is an agreed-upon list of the activities necessary to get a product increment to a done state by the end of a sprint.
44 - B	Detailing the work in the near future and keeping the items at broader details that need attention later is one mechanism to apply Progressive elaboration.
45 - D	Team story point measures can be different, and hence the team velocity of any two teams cannot be compared.
46 - INDEPENDENT, VALUABLE, SMALL	A well-written user story follows the INVEST model, developed by Bill Wake. Independent, Negotiable, Valuable, Estimable, Small, Testable. Let's see what each one means: Independent. One user story should be independent of another (as much as possible).
47 - B	Value stream mapping helps in analyzing the process and eliminating waste.
48 - B	Backlog refinement (formerly known as backlog grooming) is when the Product Owner and some, or all, of the rest of the team review items on the backlog to ensure the backlog contains the appropriate items, that they are prioritized, and that the items at the top of the backlog are ready for delivery. This activity occurs

	on a regular basis and may be an officially scheduled meeting or an ongoing activity.
49 - C	Interactive communication is the best mechanism to discuss complex issues and should be part of every communication plan. Face-to-face meeting instills trust within the team members.
50 **B-D-A-C**	The correct order for these items is as follows: 1. Sprint planning meeting 2. Daily stand-up 3. Sprint review meeting 4. Sprint retrospective meeting
Answer 51 - D	Planning poker is based on a list of features to be delivered, several copies of a deck of cards, and optionally, an egg timer that can be used to limit time spent in discussion of each item. The feature list, often a list of user stories, describes some software that needs to be developed. The cards in the deck have numbers on them. A typical deck has cards showing the Fibonacci sequence, including a zero: 0, 1, 2, 3, 5, 8, 13, 21, 34, 55, 89; other decks use similar progressions with a fixed ratio between each value, such as 1, 2, 4, 8, etc.
52 - A,B,D	A. Coach team-on-team values and Agile principles B. Make sure daily stand-ups happen and are conducted properly D. Advocate the team's position to stakeholders **Dos as a servant leader:** → Shield the team from diversions and distractions → Facilitate planning sessions → Facilitate reviews and retrospectives → Coach the team in Agile best practices → Help the team to collaborate better → Advocate the team's position → Anticipate and find ways to remove team impediments → Make sure daily stand-ups happen and are conducted properly → Encourage transparency and associated metrics → Understand and explain the team's progress to interested stakeholders

	→ Arbitrate between team members when necessary
53 - B	Forcing is win-lose. One party wins, and others lose.
54 - A,D,E	A virtual team can be more effective by increasing face-time, i.e., using tools to help teams work together, select face-to-face meetings, and interactions (by travels) to build trust, and respect all cultures and diversity. (Tip - always select the tools which involve interactions and collocation)
55 - C	The 100-point method is a prioritization method that can be used to prioritize items in a group environment. Each person within the group is given 100 points which they can distribute as votes across the available items.
56 - FALSE	A user story should have following format: As a < type of user >, I want < some goal > so that < some reason/value >. The value of the user story is missing.
57 - A	An Agile team is all about communication (usually daily), teamwork, problem-solving, technical development skills, and striving to improve the team's velocity with each iteration. Agile teams are composed of self-organized, cross-functional, highly effective groups of people
58 - B	Thumb up – Agree, Down: Disagree, Sideways - Neutral (general agreement)
59 - C	50% of 12 stories is 6 story points.
60 - A	A minimum viable product is a version of a product with just enough features to be usable by early customers who can then provide feedback for future product development. A focus on MVP development potentially avoids lengthy and unnecessary work.

PEOPLE

2.1 PEOPLE | TEAM MANAGEMENT

RECOMMENDED READINGS

PMBOK™ 6:

Chapter 3. Role Of The Project Manager and Chapter 9. Project Resource Management

OR

Pass PMP in 21 Days I – Study Guide:

Chapter 13. Team

2.1.1 QUESTIONS: PROJECT TEAM MANAGEMENT

1. You are working for a leading fashion house and managing a project named VISTA to implement a customer relationship management system. You are leading a team of more than 20 people and are currently focused on improving team performance as the team has just come on board. What are the best techniques to get your team up and ready?

    A. Collocation will help the team to be efficient due to tacit knowledge
    B. Virtual team building to share resources and non-tacit information
    C. Better conflicts management so that the team does not waste time in unnecessary fights.
    D. Assessing available skills and current trust level in your team by doing meetings and planning accordingly

2. You manage a project named VISTARA for an airline company. Since the project is in the aviation domain, a pilot, ROY, was hired as a consultant to guide the project. ROY has been working with you from the start of the project. His allocation to the project can be described as:

    A. Roy forms the virtual project team
    B. Roy was allocated to VISTARA as a pre-assigned resource
    C. Roy was allocated to VISTARA as one of the key experts for consulting
    D. Roy was allocated to VISTARA by using interpersonal skills

3. You had to set up and mobilize the resource for a new hospitality project named MAX. This requires that your team be up and working within the next few weeks. There is hardly any time for hiring, so you raise a red flag concerning this in the management meeting. The management gives you the option to select people from other business units. However, the business units are not in the same building or, in some cases, in the same location. Since the need is urgent, you select available resources as per the option presented. The team MAX will be called:

    A. Enhanced team because you are a go-getter
    B. Virtual Team, because the team is from different locations
    C. Semi-virtual team, because few team members are in the same place
    D. Co-located team because you have tools available to do a live web conference

4. **High team performance can be achieved by the following: (Select 3)**
    ☐   A. Using open and effective communication
    ☐   B. Developing trust among team members

32

☐   C. By Implementing ground rules

☐   D. Avoiding conflicts in the team

5.   Which of the following is NOT a team development stage as per the Tuckman's Team Ladder?

     A.   Adjourning

     B.   Forming

     C.   Acquiring

     D.   Norming

6.   You are managing a process optimization project for your firm. The project is named CSI. CSI required team members from the process function, distributor channel, and supply management function. You had challenges getting the team on board. Finally, there is a team in place. People are still at a distance and learning about their job requirements. Ground rules are being created while the team starts on a few of the activities. Which team development would you say the CSI team is at?

     A.   Forming

     B.   Storming

     C.   Norming

     D.   Performing

7.   You are working as an onshore manager for the HR module upgrade called HRX. This is a complex upgrade and needs many team members to come together to implement and test the new functionalities. Your team often gets into arguments about the features and priority of the tasks. This used to be healthy, but now the work is suffering because of the team members' personality differences. Which team development stage is the HRX team as per the Tuckman ladder?

     A.   Forming

     B.   Storming

     C.   Performing

     D.   Adjourning

8.   You called for a team meeting and ensured that every team member understood the value of being on time. You discussed the need to adhere to punctuality and decided on the fine if any members violate the rule. Which technique is described above?

     A.   Ground Rules

     B.   Team charter

     C.   Team-Building activities

     D.   Management skills

9. You are managing a project called ROBO3. The team encountered a sudden issue that required an urgent resolution. So, you called for a meeting with the stakeholders. This meeting will be a conference call to present the present critical issue and discuss possible solutions. Before the meeting, you sent a detailed description of the current problem. Then, while opening the meeting, you stated the problem and elaborated on the expectation from the call. The meeting closed on time, and you were able to decide on the issue resolution steps successfully. Which skills did you apply?

    A. Servant leadership
    B. Coaching skill
    C. Motivating skills
    D. Meeting management skills

10. Rob is managing a big project named SITA. The project has more than 35 people. Since the project team was allocated to Rob recently, the team members are still at their old workstations. The workstations are far from each other and sometimes even on a different floor. The team output was satisfactory, but Rob wanted a better outcome. What can Rob do to achieve a better result from the team?

    A. Rob can create a team charter
    B. Get the team at one location
    C. Use PMIS
    D. Take the team for a team-building day out

11. The project team might go through several peaks of conflict during the project life cycle. The most common sources of conflict are _____.

    A. PMO, senior management, and salaries
    B. Scarce resources, preferences, and personal work styles
    C. Resources and priorities along with rewards
    D. Team building, team combination, practical coordination, and customer

12. Your team is spread across the globe. A few team members are based in the USA, a few in India, and the rest in Japan. After many deliberations and planned decisions, the team structure and location selection were done. How would you ensure that the team focuses on the project and fully understands the project objectives?

    A. Exercise power and authority
    B. Establish a reward and recognition system
    C. Obtain the support of functional managers in other locations
    D. Have efficient and effective communications

13. You are a senior manager in an IT firm. A new bonus structure has been announced, which will impact all the employees across the region. There seems to be confusion about the way the bonus was structured. All the senior management was briefed about the bonus structure so that you can solve any question which may come along. However, when your team approached you, you referred them to HR. Which conflict resolution technique did you use?

    A. Withdraw/Avoid

    B. Smooth/Accommodate

    C. Compromise/Reconcile

    D. Force/Direct

14. The ALL-HANDS meetings are open meetings in the organization called Sapiens. These meetings are conducted once a quarter when senior management briefs employees about the focus of current projects and any upcoming changes and answers any queries from the team. Responding to one question during a recent meeting, the senior manager Steve remarked, "This is how we do things here – that's it, and I do not want to listen to any more discussion on this point," Which conflict resolution did Steve chose?

    A. Withdrawal

    B. Smoothing

    C. Compromise

    D. Forcing

15. A husband and wife both wanted to see a movie. After much deliberation, the wife won, and both saw the movie of the wife's choice. Which conflict management technique is used in this scenario?

    A. Withdraw

    B. Smooth

    C. Compromise

    D. Force

16. Sally's project team listens to her and works as per her commands. Sally has a proven track record of managing complex projects and delivering them successfully over the last 20 years. Which power influences the team most?

    A. Legitimate power

    B. Expert power

    C. Reward power

    D. Referent power

17. **You work in a matrix organization. Whom would you seek resources from?**

    A. Functional manager

    B. Program manager

    C. The PMO

    D. Other Project Managers

18. **Different people are driven by different things like power, affiliation, or achievement. This is:**

    A. Maslow's Hierarchy of needs

    B. Herzberg Motivation-Hygiene Theory

    C. McGregor's Theory X and Theory Y

    D. McClelland's Achievement Theory

19. **One of the key personality traits of successful Project Managers is delegating the work and trusting their team. A few managers do not trust their team and hence micro-manage. The theory is:**

    A. Maslow's Hierarchy of needs

    B. Herzberg Motivation-Hygiene Theory

    C. McGregor's Theory X and Theory Y

    D. McClelland's Achievement Theory

20. **Your team is formed of contributing members from various functions. Each team member generally has a few core responsibilities being part of a function and are only allocated to you on a percentage or hourly basis. There have been instances when a team member denies remembering any task allocation and blames it on other departments/persons. Which tool can help you to resolve this problem?**

    A. Team charter

    B. RACI chart

    C. Emails

    D. Meetings

21. **If You work in a Projectized organization, who would you seek resources from?**

    A. Functional manager

    B. Program manager

    C. The PMO

    D. Other Project Managers

22. Noah is managing a few people for one of an assignment. Since people are highly qualified, he lets everyone make their plans and handle any situations. Noah has given team members the authority to address any issues and circumstances. He only asks to be involved when necessary and sends weekly updates. Noah's management style can be categorized as:

    A.   Autocratic

    B.   Coaching

    C.   Directing

    D.   Laissez-faire

23. Ria is a new manager and finds managing some of her team members challenging. The team currently lacks trust and is unable to operate as one unit. Sometimes she feels that few team members question her competency and want to prove her wrong whenever they get any opportunity. What should Ria do?

    A.   Ask the functional manager to help with the replacement of the troublesome team members

    B.   Escalate the issue and let the senior manager discuss with the team

    C.   Implement the ground rules

    D.   Plan one-on-one discussions with the team to understand the issues and get feedback

24. Ethan, a young manager, seems to be everywhere and doing everything right. He has a lot of energy and gets things done. He is the youngest manager so far. There have been talks of him leading a merger project though he has never worked on such assignments before. Management seems to be confident about him doing the merger successfully. This is because of:

    A.   Ethan is PMP certified and knows to manage projects

    B.   Ethan is using networking to get ahead in the organization

    C.   Halo effect could be a possible explanation for Ethan's promotions

    D.   Young people do the work well

25. One of these techniques for building consensus where the agreement is shown using fingers and fist is called:

    A.   Fist of Five Technique

    B.   Roman Voting

    C.   Dot Voting

    D.   Polling

26. _____ is the ability to identify, assess, and manage the personal emotions of oneself and other people, as well as the collective emotions of groups of people.

    A. Emotional Intelligence
    B. Leadership
    C. Management
    D.   Intelligence Quotient

27. Negotiation is:

    A. Aimed at reaching an agreement
    B. Aimed at winning the argument
    C. Aimed at getting your things done
    D. Aimed to make people happy

28. As per Herzberg, motivating factors are: (Select 2)

    ☐   A. Salary and extra perks
    ☐   B. Authority
    ☐   C. Affiliation at the workplace
    ☐   D. Challenging work
    ☐   E. Rewards

29. For James, work is his life. He has lots of friends in the office, and he gets the job done in minutes. If you are walking with James, you will never reach the destination on time because he invariably meets people from other teams in corridors, and those talks never seem to end. All love him, and he seems to relish this fact. How would you classify James?

    A. James is driven by the affiliation
    B. James is work-oriented
    C. James is introvert
    D. James is x style of manager

30. The team SPARTA is working as a well-organized unit. Everyone is working and enjoying their work. The team hangs out in the evenings and plans for dinners together. The work seems to be progressing at an excellent pace. As per the resource plan, a few new testers joined the team. What would be the team stage at this point?

    A. Storming, the new team members will induce conflicts
    B. Performing, team stays in the same stage as before
    C. Norming, the team moves to one step earlier since there are new entrants
    D. Forming, the team moves to forming stage due to new members

2.1.2 ANSWERS: PROJECT TEAM MANAGEMENT

Answer	Why
Answer 1 - D	All the choices seem like good ones. However, one option does not fit all the scenarios. Your team is different, and the environment is different. You need to assess the team, their trust, and skills and accordingly plan to develop the team.
Answer 2 - B	Roy being a pre-assigned resource to the project, is most correct.
Answer 3 - B	Virtual teams can be defined as groups of people with a shared goal who fulfil their roles with little or no time spent meeting face to face. If your team comprises people from various locations, you need a robust communication plan.
Answer 4 - A,B,C	A. Using open and effective communication: TRUE B. Developing trust among team members: TRUE C. By implementing ground rules whenever the team meets: TRUE D. Avoiding conflicts on the team: FALSE
Answer 5 - C	There is no such term called 'acquiring' in the Tuckman ladder, and hence it is not a valid answer.
Answer 6 - A	Forming - This phase is where the team meets and learns about the project and their formal roles and responsibilities. Team members tend to be individualistic and not as open in this phase.
Answer 7 - B	Storming - During this period, the team addresses the project work, technical decisions, and the project management approach. The environment can become counterproductive if team members are not collaborative and open to differing ideas and perspectives.
Answer 8 - A	Ground rules set clear expectations regarding acceptable behavior by project team members. An early commitment to clear guidelines decreases misunderstandings and increases productivity.
Answer 9 - D	Meeting management skills.
Answer 10 - B	Co-location, also called a "tight matrix," involves placing many or all of the most active project team members in the same physical place to enhance their ability to perform as a team. The best way to get a team to be more productive is to get them in the same place.

Answer	Why
	Having people/teams together leads to trust, and improved communication leads to a better outcome.
Answer 11 - B	Conflict is inevitable in a project environment. Sources of conflict include limited resources, scheduling priorities, and personal work styles. Team ground rules, group norms, and solid project management practices, like communication planning and role definition, reduce the amount of conflict.
Answer 12 - D	What we see in the scenario is a virtual team. There are some disadvantages associated with virtual teams, such as the possibility of misunderstandings, feelings of isolation, difficulties in sharing knowledge and experience among team members, and the cost of appropriate technology. Communication planning becomes increasingly important in a virtual team environment. Planning a pull-based system, Interactive meetings, and sliding windows can help the team connect and solve the issue. Additional time may be needed to set clear expectations, promote communication, develop protocols for resolving conflict, including people in decision making, understand social differences, and share credit for successes.
Answer 13 - A	Withdraw/avoid - Retreating from an actual or potential conflict situation; postponing the issue to be better prepared or fixed by others.
Answer 14 - D	Force/direct - Pushing one's viewpoint at the expense of others; offering only win-lose solutions, usually enforced through a power status to resolve an emergency. No more discussions is forcing attitude.
Answer 15 - D	Wife won – Win-lose - forcing
Answer 16 - B	Expert power is the most lasting power and can be used most effectively to influence people. People listen to you if they know that you are an expert in the area.
Answer 17 - A	If you work in a matrix organization, people report to functional managers. When a project starts, the PM seeks resources from functional managers.

Answer	Why
Answer 18 - D	Need theory, also known as the three needs theory, proposed by psychologist David McClelland, is a motivational model that attempts to explain how the needs for achievement, power, and affiliation affect the actions of people in a managerial context.
Answer 19 - C	McGregor's Theory X and Theory Y is about managers trusting the team vs. micromanaging.
Answer 20 - B	A RACI chart is a helpful tool to use when the team consists of internal and external resources to ensure transparent divisions of roles and expectations.
Answer 21 - C	In the case of a projectized organization, the resources report to the PMO when they are not allocated to any project (they have no home/function). Some organizations have a specific department called an RMG or resource management group, which does this job. Per PMBOK, the RMG function is a specialized arm of PMO.
Answer 22 - C	In the projectized organization, the resources report to the PMO after the project completion. In some organizations, this function is a specialized unit, also referred to as a resource management group, i.e., RMG.
Answer 22 - D	Laissez-faire leadership, also known as delegation leadership, is a type of leadership style in which leaders are hands-off and allow group members to make decisions.
Answer 23 - D	A team cannot be effectively managed until a manager understands the team's aspirations and goals so they can motivate the team accordingly.
Answer 24 - C	The Halo effect is The tendency for an impression created in one area to influence opinion in another area. Example: "The ads have had a halo effect on international services."
Answer 25 - A	The Fist to Five is a technique for quickly getting feedback or gauging consensus during a meeting. The leader makes a statement, then asks everyone to show their level of agreement with the information by holding up some fingers, from 5 for wild enthusiasm down to a clenched fist.

Answer	Why
Answer 26 - A	Emotional intelligence is the ability to identify, assess, and manage the personal emotions of oneself and other people, as well as the collective emotions of groups of people.
Answer 27 - A	Negotiation is aimed at reaching an agreement. Not to win an argument, not to get your things done.
Answer 28 – D, E	Per Herzberg, the motivating factors are: challenging work, rewards, and recognition.
Answer 29 - A	James is a person who is driven by affiliation per the theory of needs presented by McClelland.
Answer 30 - D	Whenever a new member joins the team, the team moves to the forming stage.

2.2. PEOPLE | STAKEHOLDER MANAGEMENT

RECOMMENDED READINGS

PMBOK™ 6:

Chapter 13. Project Stakeholder Management

OR

Pass PMP in 21 Days I – Study Guide:

Chapter 11. Stakeholders

2.2.1 QUESTIONS: PROJECT STAKEHOLDER MANAGEMENT

1. Roy has managed the project PICCASO for the last few months. The project reports show no red flags, and customers have been quiet. Yesterday, Roy received a formal notification to him and his manager about some pending work with the project team. According to Roy, the work will be finished soon, which was conveyed to the customer. How should Roy handle the formal notice?

    A. Roy should prepare a formal note along with minutes of the discussion on the delayed work package
    B. Since the issue is escalated, let senior management respond to the issue
    C. Send the progress report to the client showcasing that the project is on track
    D. Fix up a meeting with the customer to understand the issue

2. When is the right time to perform stakeholder analysis in a project?

    A. Only at the time of project planning
    B. Throughout Project Life Cycle

3. To achieve more extensive involvement of the project stakeholders, which is the best approach one should use?

    A. Have the stakeholder's touchpoints periodically, leading to stakeholder analysis and plan ahead
    B. Invite the stakeholders to attend daily project stand-ups
    C. Send the status report to all stakeholders
    D. Regularly update the stakeholders about all project changes

4. You took over an ongoing project from Don. As per the handover routine, you started meeting with all the stakeholders. Some stakeholders you met were willing to join/help in the project requirement clarifications or building/ reviewing the product. How would you categorize the above stakeholders?

    A. Resistant
    B. Neutral
    C. Supportive
    D. Leading

5. Dennis, the marketing manager, came to see you and said that he would ensure that I, along with my project, will be closed and forgotten in the coming weeks. Dennis is _____ stakeholder.

    A. Leading

B. Supportive

C. Neutral

D. Resistive

6. **Select the odd one out:**

   A. Stakeholder identification information

   B. Stakeholder assessment information

   C. Stakeholder classification

   D. Stakeholder engagement plan

7. **There are ad-hoc information requests from Amy's supervisor, especially when Amy is about to leave for the day. Looking at trends, Amy started sending a daily digest which the supervisor did not like. Amy is having problems with these ad-hoc information requests. What would be your suggestion for Amy?**

   A. Amy can approach legal as this fall under moral harassment

   B. Amy can seek a meeting with the supervisor to understand the information needs and structure the project communications accordingly

   C. Amy should not have stopped sending those daily digests. She should again start sending the reports

   D. Do nothing. This is just a phase and will pass

8. **What is a recommended method to manage a stakeholder who is high in power and highly interested in your project?**

   A. Keep Satisfied

   B. Manage Closely

   C. Keep Informed

   D. Monitor

9. **The Identify Stakeholder is about:**

   A. making relevant information available to stakeholders as planned

   B. Determining project stakeholder information needs and defining a communication approach

   C. Identifying all people or organizations impacted by the project and documenting relevant information regarding their interest, involvement, and impact on project success

   D. Communicating and working with stakeholders to meet their needs and address issues as they occur

10. Which documents should you refer to understand the communication needs and interest level of the stakeholders?

    A. Stakeholder Register, Communication Plan
    B. Stakeholder Analysis, Stakeholder Register
    C. Communication Plan, Stakeholder Analysis
    D. Reporting Systems, Stakeholder Analysis

11. When is the right time to invite appropriate stakeholders and get their buy-in for the project objectives?

    A. While initiating
    B. At the start of the planning
    C. After creating high-level plans
    D. At the time of project closing

12. Which document would describe the stakeholder's current engagement levels and desired engagement levels:

    A. Stakeholder analysis
    B. Stakeholder register
    C. Stakeholder Management Plan
    D. Communication Plan

13. Select the TRUE statement

    A. T shaped person has broad skills across many areas but also deep expertise in one particular topic
    B. T shaped person has broad skills across a few areas (the horizontal part of the T), and deep expertise in many topics (the vertical piece)

14. The _____ establishes clear expectations regarding acceptable behavior by project team members. Early commitment to clear guidelines decreases misunderstandings and increases productivity. Discussing areas such as codes of conduct, communication, decision making, and meeting etiquette allows team members to discover values that are important to one another.

    A. Project Plan
    B. War room declarations
    C. Team charter
    D. Project Memos

15. The salience model describes classes of stakeholders based on the following, Except:

A. Power

B. Urgency

C. Legitimacy

D. Ownership

16. You instructed all the participants to think about ideas and write them the meeting. Which method did you use?

A. Workshop

B. Brainstorming

C. Meeting management

D. Brainwriting

17. You met with Kevin to discuss the project MARTHA in a pre-scheduled monthly meeting with the divisional head. The meeting went on for quite some time. Kevin seemed excited about the project work and told you that he would like to be updated on all the key milestones. Kevin emphasized that project MARTHA is a significant project for the company and can positively influence the group. How would you classify Kevin's attitude, and how would you plan to manage him?

A. Optimistic, send daily reports

B. Interested, send daily reports

C. Interested, update him often, maybe over call or mail and build the trust level

D. Trusting, update him often

18. Diana managed a massive organization-wide project named ALIVE and directly reported to the organization's COO (Chief operating officer). Project ALIVE aims to create/streamline applications and processes to monitor all the applications in real-time and provide the customers with a live simple dashboard mobile application. When you approached the COO to ask for some clarifications, he referred Diana to the functional manager, Ivan. Diana was further instructed to work closely with Ivan for day-to-day guidance. The COO instructed Diana not to disturb him for any updates, as he would get it from Ivan. How should Diana infer this conversation?

A. The COO is uninterested and should not be disturbed

B. The COO is high in power but low in interest

C. Always copy the COO in all her emails so that the COO knows that Diana is putting her best into the project

D. Work with Ivan and occasionally check with the COO for any information needs or for major project updates

19. Stakeholders can be categorized using, except:

    A.   Interest: A person or group can be affected by a decision related to the project or its outcomes.

    B.   Moral rights, such as occupational health and safety, may be defined in the legislative framework.

    C.   Salient. Provision of funds or other resources, including human resources, or providing support for the project

    D.   Contribution. Provision of funds or other resources, including human resources, or providing support for the project

20. Joe was assigned a new project by the group head of POPSCO. The group head allocated 2 resources to Joe and asked Joe to optimize the mail delivery system within the office. What should Joe do next?

    A.   Understand the office mail delivery mechanism

    B.   Get into a brainstorming workshop with 2 resources

    C.   Identify all the stakeholders of the assigned project

    D.   Create a charter

21. The project aims to provide predictive reports based on the historical sales data of the products sold in the past few years. Phase-1 of the project is complete, with some sets of reports going live. Phase-2 of the project will be launched only after checking the effectiveness of the advertising strategy based on the Phase-1 report. After much deliberation by senior management, Amy was given a green signal to start Phase-2. What should be the next step for Amy?

    A.   Amy should check the stakeholder register for any updates

    B.   Amy should check the scope of the project and verify it again, just to be sure

    C.   Amy should call for a Phase 2 kick-off meeting

    D.   Amy should create the plan for Phase-2 in detail

26. Select the correct statement

    A.   Upward influence is the influence on the senior management, customer organization, sponsor, and steering committee

    B.   Inwards influence is the influence of the team or contract workers.

22. The Phase-2 reports are mainly getting developed for the marketing function. Joe is the point of contact for marketing. Joe, being a junior executive, must get approval from his supervisor, Steve, for scope finalization. Steve is busy and takes care of marketing and sales processes and generally believes in empowering his managers. Amy requested a meeting with Steve to

get his perspective on the Phase 2 scope. Steve gave 15 minutes to Amy, where he gave a precise overview of how his team makes decisions on product advertising based on reports which are to be generated by Amy's group. These reports are currently outsourced, and a lot of money is being spent to get them refreshed. Data security is another issue for Steve. He also affirmed that the project APR is crucial to his team's overall success, and he is available for any critical decisions. Day-to-day work and reporting will be looked at by Joe. How would Amy describe Steve as a stakeholder?

- A.   Steve shows no interest in the project
- B.   Steve is an active stakeholder
- C.   Steve is supportive of the project
- D.   Steve is a neutral stakeholder

23.   To proceed further on the requirement, you asked Steve to suggest all the people who would need data from the APR project. These people are called for the requirement workshop by Amy. Amy instructed all the participants to prepare and align their thoughts and write them as a note before joining the workshop. Which method did Amy use?

- A.   Workshop
- B.   Brainstorming
- C.   Meeting management
- D.   Brainwriting

24.   Amy wanted Steve to be much more engaged with the project APR. However, Steve was very busy with his core tasks. Moreover, Steve's information needs are met by the outsourced application. From Steve's perspective, he is fine with either the outsourcing agency (Which, by the way, is very expensive) or the current initiative if they can generate the correct reports. What should Amy note for Steve in the stakeholder register?

- A.   Current engagement level: Neutral; Desired engagement level: Resistant
- B.   Current engagement level: Resistant; Desired engagement level: Leading
- C.   Current engagement level: Neutral; Desired engagement level: Supportive
- D.   Current engagement level: Resistant; Desired engagement level: Supportive

25.   Select the correct statement

- A.   Upward influence is the influence on the senior management, customer organization, sponsor, and steering committee
- B.   Inwards influence is the influence of the team or contract workers.

26. Select the stakeholder who is currently resistant and planned to be supportive as per the stakeholder register given below:

Name	Unaware	Resistant	Neutral	Supportive	Leading
Stakeholder 1		C		D	
Stakeholder 2			C	D	
Stakeholder 3				C	D
Stakeholder 4	C		D		
Stakeholder 5		C	D		
Stakeholder 6		C			D

A. Stakeholder 2

B. Stakeholder 1

C. Stakeholder 4

D. Stakeholder 5

27. Project stakeholders are, except:

A. Individuals, groups, or organizations who may affect

B. Individuals, groups, or organizations who may perceive themselves to be affected by the decision, activity, or outcome of a project.

C. Whose interests may be positively or negatively affected by the execution or completion of the project

D. Whose is not affected by the execution or completion of the project

28. Amy wanted to finalize one report with the marketing team headed by Steve. There seems to be a difference of opinion on the report format. Amy suggested voting. Six team members said OK for the current format, while the other four team members wanted changes in the current format. Select the correct answer keeping the scenario in mind:

A. Majority, report not selected

B. Plurality, report not selected

C. Unanimity, report not selected

D. Autocratic, report not selected

29. Since all members could not come to one decision, Amy resorted to their boss Steve. Steve looked at the current reports and gave a final sign-off. Which decision-making technique was used?

A. Majority, report selected

B. Plurality, report selected

C. Unanimity, report selected

D. Autocratic, report selected

30. A significant organizational change was announced. Your team reporting relationship was changed to internal communications, which is headed by David. What would be your response?

    A.   Get the requirement validated with David

    B.   Start sending status reports to David

    C.   Setup a meeting with David to explain the project

    D.   Update the stakeholder register and initiate the next steps

31. When you met with David, he asked you to involve him in daily updates. David seemed keen to shift to a new reporting system using APR. He also volunteered to test some of the reports. How would you describe your current engagement level with David?

    A.   Neutral

    B.   Positive

    C.   Supportive

    D.   Leading

2.2.2 ANSWERS: PROJECT STAKEHOLDER MANAGEMENT

Answer	Why
Answer 1 - D	PMI Tip – whenever you have an option to meet or call – choose that from all the available answers (Interactive communication) is the best mechanism to resolve any conflict/issues.
Answer 2 - B	Stakeholders are added and changed throughout the project life cycle.
Answer 3 - A	Stakeholder management, people management, schedule/cost/quality management – all tasks are to be planned and managed throughout the project life cycle. Never choose once or at controlling or planning.
Answer 4 - D	Leading stakeholders - Aware of the project, potentially impactful, and actively engaged or willing to engage towards project success.
Answer 5 - D	Dennis is a resistive stakeholder.
Answer 6 - D	Stakeholder identification, Classification, and assessment are part of the stakeholder register and can change. The stakeholder plan is an odd one here. Any planning document generally contains information like how and when, etc. Typically, these are the things that do not change. Anything that changes, like issues, risks, etc., should be contained in a register that can be referred to by the plans.
Answer 7 - B	This is an interesting question, and most of you would have faced this scenario. Do not be emotional. Work with stakeholders to understand their information needs and plan communications accordingly.
Answer 8 - B	High power and high interest should be managed closely. Build trust, communicate often, and seek help/advice to work closely with these stakeholders.
Answer 9 - C	Identifying stakeholders is about identifying people or organizations impacted by the project and documenting relevant information regarding their interest, involvement, and impact on project success.

Answer 10 - A	Stakeholder register = Interest level, authority level, and stakeholder analysis Communication Plan = for communications
Answer 11 - C	At the time of this meeting, you should have identified the stakeholders – obviously ☺. Should have a plan/schedule and other points to discuss. So the best time is after one level of planning is done.
Answer 12 - B	The stakeholder register contains all the stakeholder information.
Answer 13 - A	T-shaped skills describe specific attributes of desirable workers. The vertical bar of the T refers to expert knowledge and experience in a particular area, while the top of the T refers to an ability to collaborate with experts in other disciplines and a willingness to use the knowledge gained from this collaboration.
Answer 14 - C	The team charter establishes clear expectations regarding acceptable behavior by project team members. A guideline on codes of conduct, communication, decision making, and meeting etiquette allows team members to know and behave in the required manner.
Answer 15 - D	The salience model describes classes of stakeholders based on assessments of Power, Urgency, and Legitimacy. Ownership is not the correct dimension.
Answer 16 - D	Writing notes before joining a meeting to facilitate better brainstorming is called brainwriting.
Answer 17 - C	Kevin has a position of authority and shows high interest. The best thing to do would be to manage him closely.
Answer 18 - D	D is the best answer. Other answers seem fine as well, but working with senior stakeholders and pulse check in a while (interactive communication) – is always a good answer.
Answer 19 - C	The salient/salience model is a specific way to manage the stakeholders and is not a category of stakeholders.
Answer 20 - C	Identify the stakeholders and then start brainstorming, planning, and firming out the requirements, etc. Joe is a doer, i.e., PM does not create a charter.

Answer 21 - A	Identifying stakeholders is the FIRST thing to do whenever a new phase or new project starts.
Answer 22 - C	Steve is supportive and is high in authority.
Answer 23 - D	Writing notes before joining a meeting to facilitate better brainstorming is called the brainwriting technique.
Answer 24 - C	The current engagement level is neutral (he is OK with any method), and as a PM, you would want the high-authority stakeholder to be more involved in the project, so being supportive is the best choice to select.
Answer 25 - A	The correct answer is: upward influencing is influencing the senior management of the performing organization or customer organization, sponsor, and steering committee (Senior to the PM level(B is wrong as contractors are outside the organization.
Answer 26 - B	Stakeholder 1 Is currently resistant. The desired state is supportive.
Answer 27 - D	Project stakeholders are individuals, groups, or organizations who may affect, be affected by, or perceive themselves to be affected by a decision, activity, or outcome of a project. People who may not get affected by the project may not be a stakeholder.
Answer 28 - C	See – this is about the voting and decision-making process. 6 out of 10 are in favor. If Majority is the decision-making process, then the report should have been selected. The same goes for plurality (major set of people). But we see that the report is NOT selected, which means all should have been in favor for the report format to be approved. The decision-making criteria are UNANIMOUS. 100% agreement.
Answer 29 - D	One person made the decision – an autocratic decision-making technique.
Answer 30 - D	Stakeholders will change throughout the project life cycle. The first thing is to identify all the stakeholders in case of organizational changes or customer organization changes and then initiate the next steps like meeting and sending reports.
Answer 31 - D	David is ready to perform testing and is very keen to adapt to the new project. These are traits of a leading stakeholder.

2.3 PEOPLE | COMMUNICATIONS MANAGEMENT

RECOMMENDED READINGS

PMBOK™ 6:

Chapter 10. Project Stakeholder Management

OR

Pass PMP in 21 Days I – Study Guide:

Chapter 12. Communications

2.3.1 QUESTIONS: PROJECT COMMUNICATIONS MANAGEMENT

1. Banners are put up across the city for the upcoming national event. Banners are _____ of communication?

    A. Push method

    B. Pull method

    C. Interactive method

    D. Effective Method

2. Select the TRUE statement:

    A. Body language is a type of non-verbal communication

    B. Non-verbal communication is body language

3. Which of the following is not a valid hierarchical communication type:

    A. Horizontal

    B. Upwards

    C. Downward

    D. Vertical

4. You had 10 members in your team apart from you. 2 customer contacts are provided to seek and obtain information from the 5-member executive council. How many communication channels are present in the above scenario?

    A. 153

    B. 136

    C. 66

    D. 78

5. You are creating minutes of meeting (MOM) for the steering meeting held last week. The MOM needs to be circulated to all the internal senior management. This communication can be classified as:

    A. Internal – formal

    B. Internal - informal

    C. Official - formal

    D. Official -informal

6. RAINBOW is a project to study the environmental effect of the GM crop on human body fat composition. The project RAINBOW had accumulated lots of historical data from the project's inception. This data is often required by the subject matter experts (SME). How should you plan project communications for the effective exchange of historical data?

    A. Plan for the status meeting where the historical data can be discussed
    B. Create a repository for historical data with appropriate access to SMEs
    C. Create a configuration management plan
    D. Create a war room with all the data accessible in the war room

7. You are managing an upgrade project called TIMESHEET9. Since the project team is shared with other upgrades or new initiatives, you always have an understaffed project team. With this situation in the project, your forecast is at least 2 weeks delay in the project milestone. You are creating the status report of the project. What will you write in the project schedule status?

    A. Yellow color, the project is behind schedule
    B. Green color, the project is on schedule
    C. No color. You don't know if the project will ever be completed
    D. Red color, the project is behind schedule and now needs some external help

8. You and your team from project REALFIVE are attending a mandatory training session on leadership skills. One of the team members, Jay, joined late. There was an important discussion going on, so you asked Jay to quietly take a seat using a gesture. Which type of communication did you do?

    A. Written
    B. Verbal
    C. Non-verbal
    D. Para-lingual

9. The project EDU5 was created to streamline the registration process for an esteemed university. The core team needed to make many decisions while designating the new registration workflow and decision points. This required discussion from all the stakeholders like the core technical group, college representatives, and the student and parent bodies. The communication planning for the project EDU5 should focus on?

    A. Interactive communication
    B. Push communication
    C. Pull communication
    D. Written communication

10. A good written or spoken message should focus on:

    A. Correct grammar, concise message, clear purpose, coherent and controlled flow of ideas.

    B. Listening actively, awareness of cultural differences, and managing stakeholder expectations.

    C. Internal and external stakeholders.

    D. Info-graphics and media to convey the ideas.

11. Frank is managing the project NAMEX. He is currently involved in understanding the issues and changing the communication plan. One of the issues which are fairly recurrent and expressed by many stakeholders is that they don't know what's going on with the project. What should Frank do next? (Select 2)

    ☐ A. Update the report formats

    ☐ B. Update the communication plan

    ☐ C. Update the stakeholder register with new information on stakeholder interest

    ☐ D. Do nothing. This is normal.

12. An organization-wide initiative is underway to streamline operations and get the required quality certificate. The project is urgent and requires immediate resolution to any issue. You, as Project Manager, created task forces and planned for daily meetings. These daily meetings are quick stand-up meetings to plan for the day, understand and remove any bottlenecks and remain alert for any risks. These meetings use a war room. The war room has specific boards which capture current progress, issues, and next steps with the owner's names. Which type of communication is happening in daily meetings?

    A. Formal written

    B. Informal written

    C. Formal verbal

    D. Informal verbal

13. While addressing the concern raised by one of the team members, you shook your head, raised your eyebrow, and slowly muttered, "Really?". To which the other member smiled. Classify this communication

    A. Body language

    B. Para-lingual

    C. Informal

    D. Interactive

14. An effective communication comprises of _____, _____ and _____.

   A. Planning, doing, controlling

   B. Planning, controlling, feedback

   C. Participating, Listening, feedback

   D. Thinking, talking, controlling

15. A few factors worth considering while creating a communication plan are the following EXCEPT:

   A. Which information should be made public or private

   B. When is the information needed

   C. How to control the information from unauthorized use

   D. How many resources are required for project activities

16. Identify upward communication activity from given scenarios:

   A. You send a status report to your team members

   B. You create a knowledge repository as per the need of your project

   C. You set up a meeting with your peers to discuss the progress

   D. You brief your senior about the project progress

17. Identify horizontal communications from given scenarios:

   A. You send a status report to your team members

   B. You create a knowledge repository as per the need of your project

   C. You set up a meeting with your fellow Project Manager to discuss the progress

   D. You brief your senior about the development of the project

18. Your team was on-premises to understand the existing process for the project MACY2. You wanted the team to brainstorm on critical process goals. To do so, you called an online meeting where members can join using phones/ laptops. What is the most effective way to ensure meeting success?

   A. Ask team members to repeat the information on the call so that you get a feedback

   B. Share agenda and circulate minutes so that people know what is required from them

   C. Share the meeting agenda, circulate a template for the process documentation and discuss any issues in filling up the process documents

   D. Ask team members to create the process template and discuss that.

19. In a communication model, the receiver is responsible to:

   A.   Encode the message so that receiver can understand the feedback

   B.   Acknowledge and provide feedback on the message

   C.   Reduce noise from the system by encouraging feedback

   D.   Make sure that he/she understands the message

20. Which type of communication takes place in daily meetings?

   A.   Formal written

   B.   Informal written

   C.   Formal verbal

   D.   Informal verbal

21. You work for the top-secret mission SKY-5. No information on the project should go outside the premises or the project team. Any information leak can result in a major advantage to other countries and can have big implications for the nation. Information security for SKY-5 is a big task, and you want to ensure that only the right people should have the right access to the required information items. What will you do to achieve that?

   A.   Encrypt all the information

   B.   Implement configuration management

   C.   Implement 5C's of communication

   D.   Implement a communication plan

22. You are the manager of an FMCG firm. Your project JAGGI2 is to create a nutritional snack to be used as a breakfast stick. You wanted to do people profiling. To do this, you floated a survey to the target audience. The surveys can be considered:

   A.   Push communication

   B.   Pull communication

   C.   Interactive communication

   D.   Verbal communication

23. Noise in any communication can be all, except?

   A.   Distraction of receiver

   B.   Variations in the perception of the receiver

   C.   Lack of knowledge

   D.   Changes in the pitch and tone of the sender

24. You just joined the project team as a Project Agile coach. You set up one-on-ones with each team member. The one-on-one interaction can be classified as:

    A. Interpersonal communication

    B. Small group communication

    C. Mass communication

    D. Social communication

25. Emma calls adhoc meetings all the time. Yesterday, there was an escalation discussion meeting. Before that, it was some issue meeting and so on. The meetings go on and on, wasting everyone's time. What is your advice to Emmat?

    A. Emma could use clear grammar while addressing the team

    B. Emma could use better time management

    C. Emma could use a better flow of ideas

    D. Emma could use clear purpose while addressing the team

26. Effective communication would involve the following, except:

    A. Effective time management

    B. Defining the purpose of communication

    C. Understanding the receiver's preferences and style

    D. Measuring effectiveness of communication

27. The emerging trend in communication management is:

    A. Using the 5C's of communication

    B. Using social media communication

    C. Creating escalation plans

    D. Implementing hierarchical focus in communication

28. Scott is the new Project Manager of the HI-5 mission. He took a handover from Ken last week. Scott compiled a few reports and now wants them to go to the intended stakeholders. Scott, being new, needs your help to find out the reporting mechanism and report recipients. Which document should he refer to for this information?

    A. Communication management plan and stakeholder register

    B. Communication management plan and stakeholder strategy

    C. Stakeholder management plan and communication register

    D. Stakeholder management plan and stakeholder strategy

29. Jack is managing the project YANA. The project has a team of 10 subject matter experts, 8 developers, and 5 testers. On a typical day, Jack receives a few emails, typically seeking some input from him. A few people seek the information on discussions in the meeting. Some request him to send the latest project plan. Some of the requests are to send historical data. Mostly, the information is with them in emails, but the team seeks the information from Jack – Just to avoid any errors. And, because sometimes they do not have the latest plan with them or they are not part of the meetings. What can you conclude from the above scenario?

A. Jack is a very helpful Project Manager

B. The team YANA is in the performing stage as per the Tuckman ladder

C. Jack can put some effort into streamlining project communication. Maybe a pull communication can help

D. Jack needs to meet his team often using interactive meetings so that all the communication needs can be solved

30. What constitutes communication skills?

A. Good grammar, clear usage of words, and error-free spellings

B. Feedback and acknowledgment by the sender

C. Implementing the 5 C's of communication

D. Competence, feedback, and nonverbal communication

2.3.2 ANSWERS: PROJECT COMMUNICATIONS MANAGEMENT

Answer	Why
Answer 1 - A	Banners are the Push method. You, as the receiver, see them everywhere and may not act on all the advertisements posted on banners.
Answer 2 - A	Body language is a type of non-verbal communication
Answer 3 - D	Per PMBOK, horizontal, upwards, and downwards are types of hierarchical communication methods.
Answer 4 - A	The total number of stakeholders = 18, according to the formula to calculate the number of communication channels, which is: Communication channels = $n(n-1)/2$, Where n is the number of people. Don't forget to count the Project Manager as one of the stakeholders.
Answer 5 - A	The MOM is to be circulated internally and to senior management (upwards) and is a type of formal communication, so the communication is internal, formal, and upwards
Answer 6 - B	Let's understand the types of communications available, Pull, push, and Interactive. If you check the choices, each choice is an example of using either pull or push or interactive communication. You should know what configuration management is. If you don't know, read up See the keywords- lots of data. Experts want to access this data at their will. **Use pull communication.**
Answer 7 - D	If the project is on schedule, Yes—the color green.
Answer 8 - C	A gesture is a communication using body language or non-verbal communication.
Answer 9 - A	Discussions and decisions require more interactive elements in the project communication plan.
Answer 10 - A	The question is indirectly asking you for the 5 Cs of communication. A is the best choice.
Answer 11 - B, C	To effectively manage communications, one needs to take corrective action if required. Here, the action is to update the stakeholder register with new information and update the communication plans if needed so that the stakeholder concerns are met.
Answer 12 - C	Formal verbal. The team meets and discusses predetermined agenda points. It's not formally written, as the team is not writing the updates individually.

Answer	Why
	Updating the whiteboard is a supplementary activity in conjunction with verbal updates.
Answer 13 - A	This is body language – focus on keywords.
Answer 14 - C	Good communication is not just talking. It is listening as well. Choice C has all the right keywords.
Answer 15 - D	Communications planning is who should have what access, Which tools to use. What methods to use (Meetings, Push, Pull), etc. The choice D is planning for resources and can not be considered communications planning
Answer 16 - D	Upward communication is communication with people who are above your title.
Answer 17 - C	Horizontal communications are people who have the same title/designation as you.
Answer 18 - C	This question requires you to find out the BEST choice. All the choices look fine and will work. However, the choice which will eliminate errors and uses the resources effectively is the best choice. Providing a template will reduce a lot of effort and streamline the team toward the required exercise(s). It's a good meeting management practice to share the agenda and discuss the issues/risks to get buy-in from the team members.
Answer 19 - B	The main task of the receiver is to acknowledge the message and give feedback. A receiver decodes a message, so choice A is not correct. Choice D is totally wrong; it is the task of the sender to ensure that the receiver understands the message and eliminates any noise in the system.
Answer 20 - C	Formal verbal. The team meets and discusses predetermined agenda points. It's not formally written, as the team is not writing the updates individually. Updating the whiteboard is a supplementary activity in conjunction with verbal updates.
Answer 21 - B	Check the keywords of the question: right people should have the right access. This is achieved by using configuration management. Now, what is configuration management?
Answer 22 - A	People think of surveys as interactive communications. No, a survey is not interactive. A survey is a push communication. Note that a survey is either an email or a paper, and the recipient can ignore to answer it. Also no real-time exchange of data.

Answer	Why
Answer 23 - D	Changes in pitch and tone of the sender are required for effective communications and are not noise.
Answer 24 - A	One-on-one is interpersonal communication.
Answer 25 - D	This is a straightforward question. Any meeting requires an agenda, action points, and next steps. A meeting should have an objective and be pre planned.
Answer 26 - A	Looks like all the choices are correct. Choice A is applicable to only some partial sets of communication and is the best answer.
Answer 27 - B	Using social media is an emerging trend in communication management.
Answer 28 - A	Scott needs to know what needs to be sent and to whom. This information can be found in the communication plan. The recipient's email, phone numbers, etc., are generally not mentioned in the communication plan. If you have been managing the project for a long, then you might have created a few groups that can be mentioned in the communication plan. If not so, then you would need to check the stakeholder register. Stakeholder strategy is used as input to create the communication plan and hence not the most relevant document to look at.
Answer 29 - C	Lots of emails asking for information shows a lack of information management. If you are gatekeeping the information, then it is not an effective use of your time. Use a tool and a process. Which process? Configuration /information management.
Answer 30 - C	Implementing the 5 Cs of communication includes all the choices A, B, and D.

BUSINESS ENVIRONMENT

3.1 BUSINESS | ENVIRONMENT

RECOMMENDED READINGS

PMBOK™ 6:

Chapter 2. The Environment In Which Projects Operate

OR

Pass PMP in 21 Days I – Study Guide:

Chapter 2. The Basics

3.1.1 QUESTIONS: BUSINESS | ENVIRONMENT

1. You work with a public listed manufacturing company as a Project Manager. Your project is to implement an Enterprise Resource Planning (ERP) System to automate 20% of the ongoing manual processes. You have a team that reports to you. A project is considered complete only when:

    A. Schedule Performance Index reaches 1

    B. Cost Performance Index reaches 1

    C. The deliverables are completed, accepted, and handed over to the customer, and the Enterprise Environmental Factors are updated and archived.

    D. The deliverables are completed, accepted, and handed over to the customer, and the Organization Process Assets are updated and archived.

2. Which role can approve the change requests?

    A. Project Manager

    B. Configuration Manager

    C. Change Control Board

    D. Configuration Control Board

3. What is a Product Backlog?

    A. Product Backlog is a detailed schedule of the project

    B. Product Backlog is a list of features to be implemented.

    C. Product Backlog is the set of requirements selected for a sprint

    D. Product Backlog is an issue list of the product

4. Identify the organization shown in the diagram:

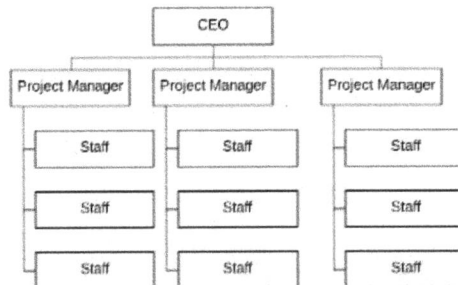

    A. Projected

    B. Functional

    C. Matrix

    D. Composite

5.   You report to the manager of program management. Your team comes from various departments, as you need several different skills sets to complete the project activities. Your team would typically report to:

   A.   Only you, the Project Manager.

   B.   Only the functional manager.

   C.   The functional manager for project work and the Project Manager for operations work.

   D.   The functional manager for operations work and the Project Manager for project work.

6.   "You are expected to keep track of status meetings, take notes, and maintain documents. If you face any problem, you should report to the engineering manager. The teams work under the assigned department, and only the manager can allocate work. The team member has one clear supervisor." These were the instructions given to you when you were appointed as a Project Coordinator for a project. What type of organization do you work with?

   A.   Projected

   B.   Functional

   C.   Matrix

   D.   Composite

7.   "You need to take full control of ABACUS, the library upgrade project. You will manage three different types of skills mainly: testers, developers, and designers. The team will report to you, and yes, It's your neck in case of any failure." This was conveyed when the project was assigned to you. What type of organization do you work with?

   A.   Projected

   B.   Functional

   C.   Matrix

   D.   Composite

8.   Every New Year comes with its security and compliance training. This training requires 2 hours per team member to complete. It is mandatory training as per the policy. The security and compliance training is an example of:

   A.   Organizational Process Assets

   B.   Enterprise Environment Factors

9. Select the scenario which depicts a project:(Select 2)

    ☐   A. Developing a new recipe for a cake. You own a cake shop.

    ☐   B. Writing a test plan for the new product.

    ☐   C. Fulfilling the new cake order. You own the cake shop.

    ☐   D. Delivering the weekly report to all stakeholders as per operation SOPs.

10. Out of the following, which of the project phases incur relatively higher costs?

    A. Starting the project

    B. Organizing and preparing

    C. Carrying out the work

    D. Closing the project

11. What is the recommended leadership style for an agile coach?

    A. Servant Leadership

    B. Authoritative Leadership

    C. Assertive Leadership

    D. Better leadership

12. Out of the following, which of the processes may incur relatively higher costs?

    A. Starting the project

    B. Organizing and preparing

    C. Carrying out the work

    D. Closing the project

13. The generic life cycle structure typically displays the following characteristics, EXCEPT:

    A. Cost and staffing levels are low at the start. They peak as the work is carried out and drop swiftly as the project moves to a close

    B. Cost and staffing levels are high at the start, they lower as the activity is carried out, and drop swiftly as the project draws to a close

    C. Risk and uncertainty are prominent at the start of the project. These circumstances decrease over the life of the project as decisions are reached and as deliverables are accepted.

    D. The ability to control the final characteristics of the project's product without significantly impacting cost is highest at the origin of the project and decreases as the project progresses towards completion.

14. "Phase to phase relationship can be overlapping or sequential." The statement is:

    A. True

    B. False

15. _____ is a method for determining user preference. In this method, different sets of users are shown similar services with one difference known as the independent variable to gather and optimize the user experience.

    A. Product Analysis

    B. Monte Carlo Simulation

    C. AB Testing

    D. Surveys

16. You refer to a few old projects and estimation guidelines to arrive at the resources estimate for your project. The guidelines and old project data which you referred to can be called:

    A. Organizational process assets

    B. Enterprise environmental factors

    C. Templates and lessons learned from project archives

    D. PMO effectiveness

17. Which project would you recommend if the selection criteria are Net Present Value? The project's data is as below:
    Project A has an IRR of 25% and an NPV of 20 million.
    Project B has an IRR of 17% and an NPV of 25 million.
    Project C has an IRR of 31 % and an NPV of 10 million.
    Project D has an IRR of 16% and an NPV of 18 million.

    A. Project A

    B. Project B

    C. Project C

    D. Project D

18. Organizational structure is _____, which can affect the availability of resources and influence how projects are conducted.

    A. Enterprise environmental factors

    B. Organizational process assets

19. A firm is divided into specialized units that host similar types of projects, e.g., Oil and Gas, Construction, Consulting, etc. The unit manager is responsible for efficiently utilizing the resources between ongoing projects. The structure can be classified as follows:

    A. Portfolio

B. Program

C. Matrix organization

D. Project

20. **A Go or No-Go decision in review meetings is typically taken by:**

A. Project Manager

B. Program Manager

C. Portfolio Manager

D. Functional Head

21. **The following are examples of EEFs (Select 2)**

☐ A. Company Infrastructure

☐ B. Issue and Defect data repositories

☐ C. Regulations

☐ D. Employee capability

22. **The project X-LABS will bring immense relief to the product packaging companies using technology and 3D rendering. However, the specifications keep changing every day. As of today, the senior management is thinking of launching a working product. The product needs to be verified and should not falter. The requirement is to go to the market with a correct product rather than to launch it ASAP. Once the user group validates the idea, addon functionalities can be launched. Which life cycle would you recommend?**

A. Predictive life cycle

B. Iterative life cycle

C. Incremental life cycle

D. Agile life cycle

23. **A need assessment involving business goals, issues, opportunities, and proposals to address them is often created. The need assessment and business case relationship are summarized below:**

A. Need assessment is created before the business case

B. Business case is prepared before need assessment

C. Business case and need assessment documents are created in parallel

D. There is no relationship between the business case and the need assessment document

24. Your team comprises of different nationalities, and they work in different time zone. What practices can help the team to be more productive?

    A.   Installing software to tack productive hours of each team member
    B.   Asking the team members to send a report every day on the work achieved
    C.   Implementing Sliding windows, Pull based knowledge repository, and clear team guidelines
    D.   Implementing push-based reporting, knowledge repository, and information radiators

25. Allowing the team to make their own decisions is one way of managing and leading a team. This style of leadership is also referred to as:

    A.   Servant leader
    B.   Interactional
    C.   Transactional
    D.   Laissez-faire

26. The customer determines that the level of risk is too high relative to the value of the requirement. So, they scoped the feature out. Which risk response was that?

    A.   Transfer
    B.   Acceptance
    C.   Mitigation
    D.   Avoidance

27. Consider the following projects with their expected Net Present Value (NPV) and Internal Rate of Return (IRR). Which of the following projects would you recommend if the selection mechanism is IRR?
    Project A has an IRR of 25% and an NPV of 20 million.
    Project B has an IRR of 17% and an NPV of 25 million.
    Project C has an IRR of 31 % and an NPV of 10 million.
    Project D has an IRR of 16% and an NPV of 18 million.

    A.   Project A
    B.   Project B
    C.   Project C
    D.   Project D

28. A process improvement initiative started in your organization. The results were efficient processes and excellent customer feedback. There are not many changes, and the team is specialized in executing the work. From the way it looks, this work will continue and will get excellence awards in the coming years. This is an example of:

    A. Excellent PMO support

    B. Great project management skills

    C. Efficient portfolio management

    D. Operation excellence

29. A group in your organization helps you with preserving the knowledge gained while executing the projects. The group also helps you with templates and other tailoring methodologies. Which is this group?

    A. Quality Management Office

    B. Project Management Office

    C. Program Management Office

    D. Excellence Office

30. An initiative, RED, is launched to build weatherproof clothing lines. RED is envisaged to be delivered in phases. The first phase requirements are fully developed to launch the summer-ware. A lot of thinking is needed to elaborate on the next step of specifications.   The customer is working towards developing the specifications for other phases but wants you to start the work as soon as possible with minimal touch-points. What would be your response?

    A. You will wait for all the specifications to be developed

    B. You will start the work using an agile approach

    C. You will start the work by selecting incremental life cycle

    D. You will start the work by selecting an adaptive life cycle

3.1.2 ANSWERS: BUSINESS | ENVIRONMENT

Answer	Why
Answer 1 - D	The project close requires that the Organization Process Assets are updated, or else the project is not considered complete. Don't get confused by Choice C, as project close does not impact EEFs typically.
Answer 2 - C	A CCB is a Change Control Board that is formed to ensure that the right decisions are made to bring about product feasibility. People who can be part of CCB are: → Influencers → Portfolio Managers (customers) → Portfolio Managers (performing organizations) → Technical architect etc.
Answer 3 - B	A Product Backlog is a prioritized list of work for the Development Team that is derived from the roadmaps and requirements. The most important items are shown at the top of the Product Backlog, so the team knows what to deliver first.
Answer 4 - A	In the given diagram, all the project team members are reporting to one manager. This manager holds the designation of a Project Manager; hence, we infer that the figure shows a projected organization.
Answer 5 -D	Observe the keywords. It says that your team is composed of people from other departments. Also, you report to a manager, and you are part of the program management vertical. This information tells us that you are part of a matrix organization. That is, your team reports to two managers. Since you belong to the management vertical, it means that the organization is a strong matrix organization, which promotes and develops project management as a domain or department.
Answer 6 - B	Do not go by the designation of the Project Manager or project coordinator. Find out how many people the team members report to. If the team members report to one boss, then the organization could be either functional or projectized. If the team reports to many bosses, then the organization is a matrix organization. Apart from the supervisor, check the authority level of the Project Manager, and then you can decide on the organization type. Here in the given scenario, the team reports to one boss,

Answer	Why
	and the project coordinator does not have much power (he is given clear directions to report to the boss). This scenario shows a typical functional organization.
Answer 7 - A	Observe the number of bosses overseeing the team and the authority level of the PM. Here in the scenario, the team reports to one manager, and the authority level of the manager is high (full control of the project). The scenario depicts a projectized organization—simple.
Answer 8 - B	Security and compliance training are mandatory per the organization's policy. This means that you cannot avoid it and have to deal with the requirement of getting people retrained. This activity limits you from performing a specific action, and there is no choice. Why is the compliance training not an OPA? See if the given activity helps you to execute your project better or not. Also, note that typically, OPAs are governed by PMO.
Answer 9 - A, B	A. Developing a new recipe for a cake; you own a cake shop. TRUE: Unique; see the keyword new recipe. B. Writing a test plan for the new product. TRUE: Unique; see the keyword new product.
Answer 10 - C	A comparatively higher number of resources is required when the actual work on the deliverables begins. This phase may be the most expensive phase of the project execution.
Answer 11 - A	With the new working style where the team is competent and self-organizing, working as a servant leader gives immense hope, trust, and outcome.
Answer 12 - C	Most of the person-hours and costs are incurred in executing processes, i.e., carrying out the work. The team develops the deliverables per the plan in execution and incurs most of the expenses.
Answer 13 -B	Understand that this is an EXCEPT question. A good way to answer this type of question is to mark each option as TRUE or FALSE. This is called the elimination technique. Let's apply the elimination technique:
Answer 14 - A	Projects can have more than one phase. Phases can be in sequence or overlapping.
Answer 15 - C	A/B testing (also known as split testing) is the process of comparing two versions of a web page, email, or other marketing asset and measuring the difference in performance. You do this by giving one version to one group

Answer	Why
	and the other version to another group. Then, you can see how each variation performs.
Answer 16 - A	Templates, estimation guidelines, and other artifacts can help you to be more efficient in your estimates or can, reduce risks on the projects or can, help you estimate better, or help your project to be more likely to succeed. Any template, guideline, estimate, lesson learned, or policy that helps you is encompassed by OPAs.
Answer 17 - B	If NPV is the selection mechanism, choose the project that has the highest NPV. In the above scenario, project B has the maximum NPV and should be selected.
Answer 18 - A	The type of structure influences the way a Project Manager carries out the work. His authority level, as well as the way resources, are organized and structured, limits the way a project can be executed. (Why limit? You cannot change the way allocations work in the organization, so you need to get the best resources with the current framework). Organizational structure is an EEF.
Answer 19 - B	In a program, the efficiencies are brought out by grouping similar projects (work). The above scenario describes the grouping of the related work to bring efficiency. So, the business units can also be called a program.
Answer 20 - C	A Portfolio Manager evaluates the ongoing portfolio components for effectiveness and can add or modify and drop components based on their value and organizational need. A project is a component of a portfolio.
Answer 21 – A, C	EEFs are the factors that you cannot change. You need to work with those aspects and plan your project. Company infrastructure and Regulations are the classic examples of EEFs.
Answer 22 - B	The keywords from the scenario are specifications that are not fully defined. A fully developed product is to be launched with each release. That points to an iterative life cycle to be selected for the project. When accuracy is important – you can select iterative development.
Answer 23 - A	Need assessment is carried out before the business case, and often the results of need assessment are summarized in business case documents.
Answer 24 - C	Using interactive tools like sliding windows and implementing information management tools (pull-based access) will help.

Answer	Why
	If you thought D is a better choice – check that it has a few good things like information radiators; however, it lacks the interactive aspects – crucial for the team to work together.
Answer 25 - D	Allowing the team to make their own decisions as one way of managing and leading a team is referred to as laissez-faire, also called the hands-off style of leadership.
Answer 26 - D	The probability of the risk is reduced to zero. The customer eliminated the risk completely. The probability of the risk is reduced to zero. This is a risk-avoid response.
Answer 27 - C	If IRR is the selection mechanism, choose the project that has the highest IRR. In the above scenario, project C has the maximum IRR and should be selected. Do not try to combine IRR and NPV combination to select the project, as that will be wrong.
Answer 28 - D	Pay attention to the keywords; the initiative has been going on, processes are matured, and the team is specialized to do the work. It cannot be project management, as the project is temporary and there needs to be risk-planning and management, but here we are talking about process maturity. This is a discussion of operational excellence. Portfolio and program management are not applicable to the scenario. Those keywords are something to think about.
Answer 29 - B	Project Management Office. The PMO is responsible for helping projects so that project management practices can be standardized, measured, and improved.
Answer 30 - C	Keywords here: the specifications for phase1 are fully developed, not many changes are required, and Minimal touchpoints. The best model to use is the incremental life cycle.

3.2 BUSINESS | INTEGRATION

RECOMMENDED READINGS

PMBOK™ 6:

Chapter 4. Integration Management

OR

Pass PMP in 21 Days I – Study Guide:

Chapter 4. Projects | Big Picture

3.2.1 BUSINESS | INTEGRATION

1. There have been many unplanned and unforeseen changes to the project UNITY. These changes were suggested by the project team and the customer. The team's morale is high, and the project status shows a CPI of 1.5 and an SPI of 1.2. The information indicates that:

   A. You are totally rocking and controlling the project well.

   B. The project performance is excellent and can't be better.

   C. The project matrix on cost and schedule is controlled, but change management could be an area to investigate and improve.

   D. The project matrix on cost and schedule is controlled, and change management is within the normal deviations and needs no further investigation.

2. **What is PESTLE?**

   A. A PESTLE is a heavy tool with a rounded end.

   B. PESTLE is a data-gathering technique to gather data on key factors (Political, Economic, Sociological, Technological, Legal, and Environmental) influencing an organization from the outside.

   C. PESTLE is a data analysis technique on key factors (Political, Economic, Sociological, Technological, Legal, and Environmental) influencing an organization from the outside.

   D. PESTLE is a used as an OPA to help the organization

3. **Select the TRUE statement (Select 2):**

   ☐ A. Tolerances are acceptable limits

   ☐ B. Control limits can be called tolerance range

   ☐ C. Tolerance range can be referred to as control charts

   ☐ D. A buffer is an example of a tolerance limit

4. **You are sending a link to the project dashboard to various stakeholders. This artifact project dashboard should be treated as (Select 2)**

   ☐ A. Information charts

   ☐ B. Project status report

   ☐ C. EEF

   ☐ D. OPA

5. You work as an offshore Project Manager for a project named SPARK. You manage the delivery and testing team. Your project has an onshore Project Manager, along with a few team members. The onshore PM works with the customer to understand, manage, and communicate project requirements, project status, and the acceptance of deliverables. You and the onshore PM report to a Program Manager, who manages a few more projects apart from project SPARK. In the above scenario, who should be responsible for creating the project plan for project SPARK?

    A. The Program Manager
    B. The Offshore Project Manager
    C. The Onshore Project Manager
    D. As per the defined Roles and Responsibility matrix

6. A management review meeting is planned for your project. You and your team prepared a status report according to the mandatory template provided by the PMO. The report is exhaustive and took all day. You compiled the project schedule, planned work items, calculated the attrition rate, project revenue, and team forecast, and identified risks and issues. Of all these actions, which is most crucial in a management review meeting?

    A. Review phase performance
    B. Authorize the changes for the next phase
    C. Applaud the project team's efforts to keep the project team morale high
    D. Authorize the project for the next phase

7. You work as a Project Manager with a national highway authority. Your project is divided into phases. The first phase, design, is the last step of execution. The design phase has a milestone called blueprint sign-off, which your team achieved today. Now is the time to initiate the second phase as per the project plan. Which of the activities below is of the lowest priority?

    A. Compiling Lessons Learned
    B. Management review and sign-off
    C. Archiving the project information
    D. Creating a roles and responsibilities matrix

8. The project charter is the document that formally authorizes the existence of a project. Who should approve the charter?

    A. Project Manager
    B. Customer
    C. Project sponsor
    D. PMO

9. Your project charter reads: "The project should be completed within one Million US dollars." According to the initial estimates, the project would cost only 80% of the proposed amount. This statement in your project would be referred to as:

   A. Project budget

   B. Project scope

   C. Management expectation

   D. Budget constraint

10. You received a change request from one stakeholder. This change was approved after much deliberation by the CCB. What is the immediate next step after the change approval?

    A. Update the traceability matrix to understand the change's impact at the end of the project.

    B. Modify the project charter to incorporate the approved changes.

    C. Have a meeting with your team to get input on the estimation of each change so that the approved changes can be incorporated into the plan and further baseline.

    D. Include the changes in the project baseline to further execute and control the changes.

11. Tacit information is (Select 2)

    ☐ A. Knowledge that can be expressed in writing

    ☐ B. Workshops or training

    ☐ C. Knowledge that is difficult to express.

    ☐ D. Personal know-how

12. What is an essential step in starting a project?

    A. To create a project plan

    B. To create a detailed scope

    C. To create a project charter/roadmap

    D. To allocate a team

13. What could be a potential threat to compliance? (Select 2)

    ☐ A. Change in legal requirements

    ☐ B. Change in regulatory policies

    ☐ C. Change in stakeholder requirements

    ☐ D. Lack of awareness of compliance requirements within the team

14.   What is the objective of creating a Project Charter?

   A.   To commit to work on the project and allocate resources.

   B.   To document enterprise environmental factors, such as stakeholders' risk tolerances and marketplace conditions.

   C.   To check historical information on the previous project. This information could be helpful since this new project is similar.

   D.   To document project statement of work.

15.   You are a Project Manager in a leading telecom infrastructure management firm. A change requested by a senior stakeholder was approved after much deliberation. What is the immediate next step for you?

   A.   Update the traceability matrix to understand the impact of the change.

   B.   Modify the project charter to incorporate the approved changes.

   C.   Have a meeting with your team to get input on the estimation of each change so that the approved changes can be incorporated into the plan and further baselined.

   D.   Include the changes in the project baseline to further execute and control the changes.

16.   Explicit information is:

   A.   Knowledge that can be expressed in writing.

   B.   Knowledge that is difficult to express.

17.   You are in the process of reviewing a document that lists the vision of an initiative and the resource requirements and business risks associated with the initiative. You decided to approve the document after due diligence. You also allocated a few resources to this initiative so that the work can start. What is your role?

   A.   Project Manager

   B.   Quality Manager

   C.   Functional Manager

   D.   Portfolio Manager

18.   Project GREY GOOSE is all about the morale of the organization. The goal is to get people's morale up by 5% in the next three months. After much deliberation by the committee, you are selected as the PM of the project. What should be the first step for you to carry the project forward?

   A.   Develop the preliminary project scope statement.

   B.   Gather information about who could be potential stakeholders.

C. Start to create a project plan.

D. Get the project charter signed.

19. Sarbanes-Oxley, Sarbox, or SOX, is the United States federal law that sets new or enhanced standards for all U.S. public company boards, management, and public accounting firms. The SOX audit was performed a few days ago. There were a few observations that resulted in changes in security processes and guidelines. Project BOOMBOX is created to close all the gaps found in the SOX audit. Project BOOMBOX was triggered due to:

A. Customer request

B. Legal requirement

C. Technological advancement

D. Business need

20. Select 2 NON-FUNCTIONAL requirements:

☐ A. The defect ratio should be less than 95%

☐ B. The transaction clearance ratio should be more than 99% Co

☐ C. The car should have a seating capacity for four

☐ D. The website should have a logo of all payment gateways

21. Select the TRUE statement about knowledge management in projects:

A. Tacit knowledge is easier to document as lessons learned and is an essential part of knowledge management.

B. Tacit knowledge is difficult to document as a lesson learned and is an essential part of knowledge management.

22. The most important part of knowledge management is to create an environment of _____ so that people are motivated to share their knowledge.

A. Competition

B. Rewards

C. Trust

D. Insecurity

23. Grey, the wise Project Manager, is managing a mixed team. He has novice members on the team, along with very senior members. The team seems to be working fine, but the efficiency of the junior members is not improving as expected. Most of the time, senior members must correct their problems. This pattern is affecting the project schedule and project deliverable quality. What should Grey do next to solve this issue?

A. Nothing. This is a normal issue that gets solved with time.

B. Initiate a formal information management system and ensure that a lesson learned document is updated after each mistake.

C. Work with senior members to provide formal training to beginners.

D. Network and listen to the team to understand gaps and facilitate information sharing during the daily activities.

24. **You are in the process of gathering all the requirements and creating the scope. You received some more requirements from a stakeholder today. You will treat the new requirements as:**

A. Additional requirements and keep them for the next phase of the project

B. Change requests, add them to the change log to be taken to the change control board for approval

C. Minor changes and rolls them out in the current phase

D. Requirements and prioritize them as part of the requirement prioritization matrix

25. **You were handed a project named VARSITY, which is aimed at a student learning system for distance learning. When you took over the project, you found that the change log has many approved change requests which are yet to be implemented. If you implement the approved changes, then the project milestones will surely be impacted. Your team is busy full-time with its current work. What is your next step?**

A. Call a team meeting to allocate extra work so that approved change requests can be implemented

B. Update the plan with approved changes and allocate work accordingly

C. Call a prioritization meeting with all stakeholders to discuss the impact of changes in the baselines and take it from there

D. Leave the implementation of approved changes until someone ask about them

26. **You were in the process of creating a plan along with your team, and there were discussions on how to arrive at the project delivery schedule and elicit full requirements from customers. You also shared a few ideas with your team. You wanted everyone to participate, so you encouraged everyone to come up with at least one talking point. Which technique did you use?**

A. Expert judgment

B. Facilitation

C. Brainstorming

D. Interviews

27. To ensure the customer understands the workflow and features, your team created a few dummy screens(wireframes). These wireframes can be classified as:

   A. Prototype
   B. Context diagram
   C. Affinity Diagram
   D. Requirements

28. _____ is used to forecast future performance based on past results.

   A. Root cause analysis
   B. Trend analysis
   C. Variance analysis
   D. Earned value analysis

29. _____ reviews the difference between planned and actual performance.

   A. Root cause analysis
   B. Trend analysis
   C. Variance analysis
   D. Earned value analysis

30. You are heading a project called MEGA ROW. The project is to monitor the current level of pollution in the Ganges River and propose a solution. Your project has various deliverables in various phases. In the first phase, you wanted to ensure that the testing team thoroughly test all the deliverables. The test results were astonishing and found a 25% defect percentage. The organization's upper limit is 15%. Your next step is to perform:

   A. Root cause analysis
   B. Trend analysis
   C. Variance analysis
   D. Earned value analysis

31. The project benefits management plan is the document that describes how and when the benefits of the project will be delivered. What are the typical components of project benefits management plan (Select 3)

   ☐ A. Target benefits
   ☐ B. Strategic alignment
   ☐ C. Benefits owner
   ☐ D. Defect metrics

32. In _____, the project scope is generally determined early in the project life cycle, but time and cost estimates are routinely modified as the project team's understanding of the product increases. Iterations develop the product through a series of repeated cycles, while increments successively add to the functionality of the product.

    A.   Iterative life cycle

    B.   Incremental life cycle

    C.   Adaptive life cycles

    D.   Predictive life cycle

3.2.2 ANSWERS: BUSINESS | INTEGRATION

Answer	Why
Answer 1 - C	In this question, it appears as if everything is fine with project UNITY, so option A or option B appear appropriate. But a closer look at the scenario shows that there are many changes in the project. In this case, the best thing to do is check the root cause. Are the changes suggested because the team was unable to capture the requirements in the first place, or is the business scenario dynamic and the project delivery approach to be changed? Choice C is most suitable, as you need to be concerned about changes and investigate them.
Answer 2 - C	A PESTLE analysis is a framework to analyze the key factors (Political, Economic, Sociological, Technological, Legal, and Environmental) influencing an organization from the outside.
Answer 3 - A, B	Think control charts and control limits, and then answer this question.
Answer 4 - B, D	Project status reports fall under the category of execution reports. These reports show the project execution status, risks, issues, and compliances that could be other heads under this report. The execution report should be archived under OPAs
Answer 5 - D	This is an interesting question. All of the choices seem to be correct. Here we need to find the BEST answer. A plan can be created by the onshore PM, offshore PM, or both, or the program manager may create an overall project plan. A good idea is to clearly write who does what in the roles and responsibilities section of the human resource management plan. This will avoid any confusion among stakeholders. So the BEST answer is D.
Answer 6 - D	This is a detailed question. You must read the entire scenario to understand which meeting is being described. The meeting described in the scenario is a phase-end review meeting. In this meeting, the Portfolio Manager/stakeholders decide whether to continue to the next phase. So, choice D is correct. If you selected Choice A, you likely rushed through the question. Calm down and consider all choices to find the best answer.
Answer 7 - D	In this question, you must single out the choices that are FALSE. First, you must understand which project stage the scenario describes. If the deliverables have been completed, you need to close the current phase and initiate the

next one. So, let's identify which of the activities should be performed to close the current phase:

Answer 8 - C	This is a tricky question. Please note that the project charter is not written by the Project Manager. The authority and responsibility lie with the project sponsor to authorize the project. As the name suggests, the project sponsor is the entity with the funds and vision for the project. Typically, a Portfolio Manager is a project sponsor in the event of a captive organization (Please read "Pass PMP in 21 Days - Study Guide" to learn more).
Answer 9 - D	You may feel that the project would cost less, but any limit (on time, resources, cost, etc.) is a constraint.
Answer 10 - C	This question tests your understanding of the change management process. Let's use the elimination technique:
Answer 11 - D	This is a direct question from PMBOK. The definition of tacit knowledge is "Knowledge that is personal and difficult to express, such as beliefs, insights, know-how, etc."
Answer 12 - C	Creating a project charter or, in the case of an agile project, a roadmap is an essential step in initiating a project. This is an initial analysis by the Portfolio Manager to understand the needs and document the expected results of the project. A charter is a commitment to allocate resources towards the project.
Answer 13 - A, B	A and B are correct options. Stakeholder requirement may change and has to be processed accordingly. Lack of compliance awareness in the team is an issue and needs to be planned for.
Answer 14 - A	A project charter contains reasons for project initiation and the expected project results. It also creates an entity in the organization with which the resources can be aligned to achieve the desired results.
Answer 15 - C	This answer tests your understanding of the change management process using the elimination technique: A. Update the traceability matrix to understand the change's impact at the end of the project - MAYBE, but let's look for a better answer. B. Modify the project charter to incorporate the approved changes - NO, not applicable as the PM is not the owner of the project charter. C. Have a meeting with your team to get input on the estimation of each change so that the approved changes can be incorporated into the plan and further baselined - MAYBE, this is a better option than A, but let's look for a better answer.

	D. Include the changes in the project baseline to further execute and control the changes - NO, although this option appears valid, a baseline is created to monitor and control a project, not the changes. By looking at all the choices above. The best choice is C.
Answer 16 - A	Explicit knowledge is the one that can be documented and shared. Tacit knowledge is in the minds and difficult to document.
Answer 17 - D	Typically, a Portfolio Manager selects the new components (e.g., projects/programs), manages the elements, and streamlines them (can kill projects) to ensure efficiency. So, the best choice would be the Portfolio Manager.
Answer 18 - B	The PM must perform all initiating processes before planning begins. Only two processes are conducted in the initiating process group: Creating a charter (where a PM's responsibilities are allocated) and initiating the process group, where stakeholder analysis (gathering information about all stakeholders to start planning for the project work, communication, etc.) is conducted.
Answer 19 - B	The project BOOMBOX is started due to legal requirements.
Answer 20 - A, B	What is a non-functional requirement? The requirements on ilities, i.e., Scalability, extensibility, performance, etc A. The defect ratio should be less than 95%. TRUE: This is a non-functional requirement B. The transaction clearance ratio should be more than 99%. TRUE: This is a non-functional requirement C. The car should have 4 person seating capacity: Is a functionality D. The website should have a logo of all payment gateways. Is a functionality
Answer 21 - B	Tacit knowledge is difficult to document as a lesson learned and is an essential part of knowledge management is a TRUE statement
Answer 22 - C	This is a straightforward question, but you might be confused by choices B and C. The best answer is TRUST. Rewards may help for knowledge management efficiency, but trust will be a key enabler.
Answer 23 - D	Understand that the question discusses knowledge management. It's important to capture tacit information from senior members of the team. This can be achieved with trust, communication, and information-sharing sessions. Choice D is the BEST choice. Choices B and C may be used to capture explicit know-how, so they are not the best choices.

Answer 24 - D	Since the project scope is not baselined yet, the new requirements should be treated as normal requirements and not changes. These requirements should then be rolled out according to the requirement urgency, and feasibility, typically called the requirement prioritization process.
Answer 25 - C	Understand that the project baselines will be changed if the approved changes are to be implemented. Since you are new, it makes sense to discuss the impact of all the approved change implantations on a plan where stakeholders are required to agree on a new plan, which may have changed timelines or updated resource requirements. While choice B may seem like the best choice, you, as PM, cannot independently change the baselines. You would need permission from the required stakeholders.
Answer 26 - C	Check the scenario for keywords. You get keywords like ideas and facilitation. Yes, you did facilitation but to generate ideas. So, the technique used is brainstorming.
	Interviews is totally wrong and hence are not a valid option.
	Expert judgment, a choice should be selected as the last choice if none of the other choices are valid since expert judgment is too broad and can be applied in any form—any process.
	So as a thumb rule, select the precise choice which fulfils all the keywords. Idea and facilitation keywords are found via brainstorming.
Answer 27 - A	Wireframes can be classified as a prototype. A prototype would help the team gather early feedback on the requirements.
Answer 28 - B	Trend analysis is used to forecast future performance based on past results.
Answer 29 - C	Variance analysis reviews the difference between planned and actual performance.
Answer 30 – A	The situation shows that defect levels are way too high and need to be investigated to determine the root cause. Note that the keywords here are "upper limit." The best thing to do is to perform an RCA analysis.
Answer 31 – A, B, C	The project benefits management plan is the document that describes how and when the benefits of the project will be delivered and describe the mechanisms that should be in place to measure those benefits. A few things to include are:

→ Target benefits (e.g., the expected tangible and intangible value to be gained by the implementation of the project; financial value is expressed as net present value);

→ Strategic alignment (e.g., how well the project benefits align to the business strategies of the organization);

→ Time-frame for realizing benefits (e.g., benefits by phase, short-term, long-term, and ongoing);

→ Benefits owner (e.g., the accountable person to monitor, record, and report realized benefits throughout the time frame established in the plan);

→ Metrics (e.g., the measures to be used to show benefits realized, direct measures, and indirect measures);

→ Assumptions (e.g., factors expected to be in place or to be in evidence); and

→ Risks (e.g., risks for the realization of benefits).

Answer 32 - A	In an iterative life cycle, the project scope is generally determined early in the project life cycle, but time and cost estimates are routinely modified as the project team's understanding of the product increases. Iterations develop the product through a series of repeated cycles, while increments successively add to the functionality of the product.

PROCESS

4.1 PROCESS | SCOPE MANAGEMENT

RECOMMENDED READINGS

PMBOK™ 6:

Chapter 5. Scope Management

OR

Pass PMP in 21 Days I – Study Guide:

Chapter 5. Scope and deliverables

4.1.1 QUESTIONS: PROCESS | SCOPE MANAGEMENT

1. You are managing a project named BBMAN. The project outcome is to develop an engaging puzzle game for iOS devices. You are concerned that the project scope keeps changing. Project scope management is primarily concerned with:

   A. Defining and controlling what is included in the product scope.

   B. Establishing what is and is not covered in the project scope.

   C. Defining and controlling what is excluded from the project scope.

   D. Defining and controlling inclusions and exclusions of the project and product.

2. You are managing a construction project for the eGOV initiative. There were a few challenges getting the right approvals, but now things seem to be settling. You planned a few meetings to get started on requirements. One meeting you planned involved getting all the legal staff together to understand the legal aspects and analyze responses. This is a:

   A. Delphi technique

   B. Focus Group

   C. Interview

   D. Facilitated workshop

3. You oversee project NXTRA. The goal of the project is to provide a uniform view and workflow to all the office employees. This will also have social capabilities to boost communication within the groups. You planned to have a workshop with all the group functional heads to gather expectations from each group. You are also aware that there are people with strong views on the subject, and it is necessary to get the discussion back on the workshop agenda to avoid any topic deviations. So you requested the CIO lead the discussion. Identify the technique that you plan to use:

   A. Delphi technique
   B. Focus Group
   C. Interview
   D. Facilitated workshops

4. Roy is tasked with finding the internal trend on the recent change in employee policy. The organization has more than 20,000 geographically separated people working in different time zones. Which technique will help Roy to get this information most efficiently?

   A. Delphi technique
   B. Surveys
   C. Interviews
   D. Mind maps

5. Your organization has recently faced a few challenges in the L2R process (Lead to Revenue). The auditors found huge revenue leakages due to gaps in the process. The CIO authorized you to investigate it and suggest a plan to decrease revenue losses by 10% in the next six months. You called a meeting of all experts to get as many ideas as possible, then selected the top three ideas to investigate further. Which technique did you use?

   A. Brainstorming
   B. Nominal group technique
   C. Interviews
   D. Facilitated workshops

6. LocalOil Corporation Ltd is one of the world's largest commercial oil and gas enterprises. The company owns and operates 20 refineries and caters to clients in aviation, railways, and retail by selling the petrol and lubes to aviation, railways, and retail outlet customers. You are the planning head for the new upcoming refinery, PARFIN. Your team created the description of the work. You also added exclusions and assumptions in the document. Which document did you create?

   A. Scope Management Plan
   B. Project Scope document
   C. Requirements Traceability Matrix
   D. Requirement Management Plan

7. What level is the "1.2 Design" WBS item in the project?

   A. Level 1
   B. Level 2
   C. Level 3
   D. Level 0

8. You are the Project Manager for project TIPTOE. Your team created a work breakdown structure (WBS) for the product and project. Which of the following is TRUE about WBS numbering?

   A. The numbering system is a unique identifier known as the code of accounts
   B. The numbering system is a unique identifier known as the WBS accounts
   C. The numbering system is a unique identifier known as the WBS dictionary accounts
   D. The numbering system is a unique identifier known as the WBS control account

9. You work at a mobile manufacturing company. The current project, LIGHTPEN, aims to develop a mobile phone which is at least 10% thinner than its current counterparts and features an auto-renewable solar battery. The idea is to release this mobile phone in the market at Christmas time. This means that it needs to be ready to market by the JULYFEST consumer fair (typically held in the third week of July), where retailers make choices about which items to buy for upcoming seasons. The team is in the process of ensuring the mobile phone meets federal safety rules, which it does, but the product is running into a problem with additional non-federal safety issues that are only now being discovered. Identify the assumption, constraint, and product description from the above scenario:

    A. Assumption: The product must be ready for the business in July; Constraint: Safety criteria; Product Description: It is a mobile phone.

    B. Assumption: National safety regulations are sufficient for a mobile phone; Constraint: The product must be market-ready by July; Product Description: A mobile phone with an auto-renewable solar battery.

    C. Assumption: The Project Manager is responsible for the product's safety results; Constraint: The mobile phone must meet national safety standards; Product Description: The product is a mobile phone.

    D. Assumption: Non-federal safety issues might come up; Constraint: The mobile phone must be sold at Christmas; Product Description: The mobile phone must appeal to retailers.

10. The Director kicked off the release of a new milestone. He was very pleased with the project's progress in later stages and has gone to the extent of saying that the current version of the product would be the one to bring innovation. You see some fears and some anxiety in the team. These people report to the Director. You thought that you might need to reach out to these experts and understand why they feel apprehensive. You created a note and sent it to all the experts and mentioned that these fears would be anonymous. Which technique did you use?

    A. Alternative identification

    B. Nominal group technique

    C. Affinity diagram

    D. Delphi technique

11. You are managing a project for the time-sheet management system TIMEFIX. Phase-1 is ongoing. You wanted to freeze the requirement for the next phase, so you called for a workshop. Fifteen experts participated in the workshop, each with a different function. Each participant felt that the features required by their department were most urgent and should be

prioritized for the next phase. According to the team capacity and planning, you can roll out only five features at most. It seemed difficult to arrive at the release sequence of the required features, as every one of the participants was too possessive and adamant about their piece of the requirement. What can help you the most?

A.   Randomly select five features for the next phase

B.   Use a nominal group technique

C.   Ask the Change Control Board to make the final decision

D.   Use the Delphi technique

12.   You are working on a process optimization initiative called LEAN. You have a target to optimize approximately 30-50 processes. The objective is to be leaner and swifter. In order to have an incremental impact within the organization, a functional group, STAYLEAN, has been formed. STAYLEAN is authorized to prioritize and initiate process changes. If you are the Project Manager for the LEAN initiative, how would you recommend rolling out new and improved changes?

A.   Using an iterative methodology

B.   Using an incremental methodology

C.   Using agile methodology

D.   Using waterfall methodology

13.   You just took over a project from an outgoing Project Manager. During the shadow period, you had a chance to be part of an acceptance meeting, which was a surprise to you and the customer. In the acceptance meeting, typically, the customer checks the deliverable and accepts it. However, this meeting was very different. When the customer checked the deliverable, they seemed surprised and commented that they did not know if this would work. The meeting somehow turned into more of a discussion on requirements. When you checked with the outgoing PM, he mentioned that this is a normal occurrence, as the customer does not know technology and is unable to envisage the outcome. You now need to take over to start working on the next phase of the project. Which tool could help you avoid last-minute changes?

A.   Use a firm change control process

B.   Be better at meeting coordination

C.   Use interpersonal and management skills

D.   Create a prototype

14. Select all the items which you can find in a status report to be sent to the Steering Committee of the project.

    ☐   A. Detailed activity completion status along with owners

    ☐   B. Milestone missed

    ☐   C. Project Issues

    ☐   D. Milestones met

15. You discover that two of your team members discussed a work package and made many changes to it during its development. The work package is now complete, and the team members are planning to go on to the next work package. While reviewing the work, you found that the work does not meet the allocated requirements of the work package. What is the BEST course of action?

    A.   Accept the work package and allocate new work

    B.   Raise a change in plan

    C.   Issue a note to the functional manager about the work quality

    D.   De-allocate people from your project

16. In agile projects, the requirements constitute the _____.

    A.   Product scope

    B.   User story

    C.   Product Backlog

    D.   Project scope

17. What is the least likely use of a requirement traceability matrix:

    A.   To link product requirements from their origin to the deliverables that satisfy them

    B.   To provide a means to track requirements

    C.   To provide an arrangement for managing changes to the product scope

    D.   To help in planning the scope

18. Scope baseline consists of:

    A.   Approved project and product scope, WBS and WBS dictionary

    B.   Approved project scope and WBS

    C.   Approved product scope and WBS

    D.   Approved project statement, WBS and WBS dictionary

19. Select the incorrect option regarding control accounts:

    A. A control account is an administration control point where scope, budget, actual cost, and schedule are integrated

    B. Control accounts are located at selected management points in the WBS

    C. Each control account may include one or more work packages

    D. A work package can be associated with more than one control account

20. Select the FALSE statements:

    A. The level of detail for work packages will vary with the size and complexity of the project.

    B. The level of detail for work packages should follow the 40-80 hours rule.

21. You are tasked with project MUNCH. The customer wants a dynamic advertisement for one of its products. This advertisement should be focused on young college students. This is the only specification you received from your customer. Things are evolving but are hazy right now. Which methodology will work best for project MUNCH?

    A. Create a prototype and refine and release versions

    B. Conduct interviews and get the best inputs from experts to build solid requirements

    C. Using an iterative approach, create an advertisement and refine it

    D. Using an incremental approach, create parts of the advertisement, showcase it to the customer and further refine it

22. What is least likely to be found in the scope management plan:

    A. A process for preparing the scope statement

    B. A process for WBS creation and guidelines associated with it

    C. A process for formal acceptance of project deliverables

    D. A process for requirement prioritization

23. You are planning for the smart city metro transport. The related project, which deals with transportation, is named CHECKPOINT. Currently, you are in the process of gathering as much information as possible on the requirements. Which of the following is not a data-gathering technique?

    A. Benchmarking

    B. Affinity diagram

    C. Focus group

    D. Surveys

24. Project SPARK was initiated, and you were given the responsibility to manage the process transition. This was a particularly difficult task, as your team did not know much about the current process. There are also transition problems, as the customer team members are hesitant to share the key process with your team. How would you plan for the requirements?

   A. You will plan interviews with SMEs, as this is the best method for understanding requirements

   B. You will plan focus groups so that every member of your team can understand the processes and ask questions

   C. Surveys will help, as they are non-intrusive, and you can get all perspectives by covering wider audiences

   D. Observations will help to see people performing on the job while your team documents the process

25. Your business analyst sent you the first version of the requirements. It contains a diagram showing the new system's interactions with other systems. This diagram is:

   A. A context diagram

   B. An affinity diagram

   C. A mind map

   D. A user story

26. As per the organization template, you divided the requirements into functional and non-functional requirements. What is a functional requirement? Select the FALSE statement:

   A. Functional requirement describes product processes

   B. Functional requirement describes product performance

   C. Functional requirement describes product data

   D. Functional requirement describes product interactions

27. Your boss asked you a question in a steering team meeting: Since the project seems to be a long-duration project, how would you ensure that your team delivers all the requirements given by the customer until project closure? What would be your response?

   A. I will ensure that we follow proper documentation of the requirements

   B. I will manage my project until it is handed over. That way, I will ensure that no requirements slip through the cracks

   C. I will use a traceability matrix

   D. I will use the requirement management plan and good acceptance testing

28. For some WBS components, which are planned, the detailing is left for the future. This can be referred to as:

    A.   Laziness

    B.   Agile methodology

    C.   Rolling wave planning

    D.   Work package

29. You are managing project JPM for an online e-commerce firm. Project JPM's scope is to develop predictive selling trends for several of the firm's products. The customer is in the process of checking the first few predictive reports. The current process can be referred to as any of the following, EXCEPT:

    A.   Reviews

    B.   Acceptance testing

    C.   Inspection

    D.   Quality testing

30. What is variance analysis:

    A.   Comparing baseline vs. actual results

    B.   Comparing planned vs. actual

    C.   Comparing planned scope to the actual product delivered

    D.   Comparing planned schedule to actual completion of the project

4.1.2 ANSWERS: PROCESS | SCOPE MANAGEMENT

Answer	Why
Answer 1 - D	Project scope creates the boundaries of the scope. The scope will list what is in/out of scope, assumptions, and constraints.
Answer 2 - B	Check that the meeting has people from one department. People from similar domains constitute a focus group.
Answer 3 - D	People from different fields, when coming together, may lead to discussions that may be dominated by strong personalities. Hence you would need someone to facilitate a discussion of the goal of the workshop. So, the answer here would be "facilitated workshop."
Answer 4 - B	Use surveys to get inputs from many geographically separated stakeholders working in different time zones in a shorter span of time.
Answer 5 - B	When you rank or prioritize the ideas, it's called the nominal group technique.
Answer 6 - B	The project scope statement contains a description of the product and project scope, inclusions and exclusions from scope, and potential sections regarding constraints and assumptions.
Answer 7 - A	A WBS contains levels. The first level is referred to as level zero. "1.2 Design" makes the first decomposition and hence is designated as level 1.
Answer 8 - A	Choices B and C are completely ruled out. A unique numbering system in WBS is called the code of accounts, so choice A is a valid one. A control account is a management control point where scope, budget, actual cost, and schedule are integrated and compared to the earned value for performance measurement
Answer 9 - B	Choices A and D are wrong straightaway. Out of choices B and C, the correct definition is in choice B, which contains a product description stating that the mobile phone has an auto-renewable solar battery. This is a better description than the product description in choice C.
Answer 10 - D	Delphi technique keywords are unbiased and anonymous. You get both of them here.
Answer 11 - B	Choices A and C are wrong straightaway. Why is choice C wrong? Since we are getting the requirement for the first time, there is no role

for CCB yet. We are in a workshop, so there is no need for a Delphi. Even Delphi may not help in prioritizing. Voting and ranking is the best technique to prioritize the requirements. Choice B is the best answer.

Answer 12 - B	The project scope is incremental and has to be implemented in incremental phases. Process 1 would be rolled out first—then process 2, and so on.
Answer 13 - D	You might be confused between choice A and choice D. If you look at the question, it asks you how you could have avoided the changes in the first place? A prototype helps capture the requirements and get the early sign-off on the approved functionalities.
Answer 14 – B,C,D	A status report contains project status at a high level. Going into details is not required.
Answer 15 - B	Choice C looks good, and you might be tempted to select it. However, you would need to ensure quality work is being allocated. So, to get good work packages with the right quality, you need to raise a change in the plan to accommodate the work.
Answer 16 - C	In Agile projects, the requirements to be developed are part of the Product Backlog.
Answer 17 - D	For this question, you need to find the statement that is FALSE for RTM. Choice D is FALSE, as RTM does not help in planning scope processes.
Answer 18 - D	Scope baseline contains the approved scope, WBS, and WBS dictionary. If you are from the Agile or IT field – Just remember the 3 artifacts. What is a scope baseline? The scope that is agreed upon and approved.
Answer 19 - D	Any question which is EXCEPT or NOT TRUE can be solved by using the TRUE/FALSE technique.

A. A control account is an administration control point where scope, budget, actual cost, and schedule are integrated - TRUE

B. Control accounts are located at selected management points in the WBS - TRUE

C. Each control account may include one or more work packages - TRUE

D. A work package can be associated with more than one control account - FALSE (since it is hierarchical, a work package should be

	associated with only ONE control account)
Answer 20 - B	The WBS details and work package elaboration depends on the project's complexity and duration of the project.
Answer 21 - A	This is the BEST ANSWER. All of the options look good; however, when you analyze further, you will be able to understand that, using options B, C, and D, you will end up making a product. In the event of changes, those changes will be costly. If the requirements are unclear, it's a good idea to get early confirmation on requirements using a prototype. You can further refine the requirements after getting inputs on the prototype. This way, the team and project save effort, changes, and time.
Answer 22 - D	Anything to deal with requirements is part of the requirement management plan. The scope management plan includes all the processes for delivering the product to the customer.
Answer 23 - B	Affinity diagrams are used to represent data.
Answer 24 - D	Everything listed above will work, but what will work best is observation. Why? In case of new, complex processes/requirements, and if there are language barriers or mental biases, then this is the best option to use observations to collect relevant information.
Answer 25 - A	A context diagram shows the system's interactions with other entities.
Answer 26 - B	Functional requirements describe the behavior of the product, e.g., processes, data, and interactions. Non-functional requirements describe the performance, and environmental conditions, e.g., reliability, performance, and security.
Answer 27 - C	A traceability matrix will help trace the requirements from the project's origin to its closure.
Answer 28 - C	Decomposition may not be relevant for future work components, and elaboration may need more details. When the elaboration is left for later stages until clarity evolves, this is referred to as rolling wave planning. It is also referred to as progressive elaboration.
Answer 29 - D	First of all, which process is being performed here? The customer performs only one function/process in PMBOK: validate scope. The customer is performing acceptance testing, which is also referred to as

a review. Inspection, walkthroughs, QC, etc., are activities that should have happened before the acceptance testing by the testing team.

| Answer 30 - A | Variance analysis is a technique used in most of the controlling processes to discover the difference between planned vs. actual results. The planned aspect could be schedule, cost, or scope—or any other parameter—and is compared with actual results. Planned data to use for comparison is always taken from the baselines, so choice A is the most sensible. The rest of the options are all correct but are incomplete. |

4.2 SCHEDULE MANAGEMENT

RECOMMENDED READINGS

PMBOK™ 6:

Chapter 6. Schedule Management

OR

Pass PMP in 21 Days I – Study Guide:

Chapter 6. Time Management

4.2.1 QUESTIONS: PROCESS | SCHEDULE MANAGEMENT

1. You are a Project Manager for the commissioning of an oil ship. The project is named MS HYDRA. While creating the project schedule, you found that a few resources were over-allocated beyond their committed hours. You analyzed the overall schedule and reduced their committed hours on the project as per the company work policy for the week. That would mean that the work was distributed to some other resources. Which technique did you use?

    A.   Resource leveling

    B.   Resource smoothing

    C.   Resource optimization

    D.   Project analysis

2. You are a Project Manager for project MAD HATTER. You received several calls in the past 2-3 days inquiring whether any of the resources can be released from the project. There were 3 more calls today. The project seems to be going at a good pace, and people seem happy. The risk rating is low. Activity A has an early start date of 4 and a late start date of 2. Activity B has a float of 3 days. Activity R has an early start date of 5 and a late start date of 15. The CPI of the project is 1.2. Most of the stakeholders seem fine with the project's progress. The procurement kicked off as per the plan. What should you do?

    A.   Crash Activity A

    B.   Crash Activity R

    C.   Think of ways to reduce the impact of phone calls

    D.   Plan procurement in detail

3. Ben is creating the project status report and updating the overall work status. While checking the schedule, he noticed that a few of the activities in the project are showing negative float. In which situation, an activity can have a negative float:

    A.   The early finish is equal to the late finish

    B.   The late start date is earlier than the early start

    C.   Crashing results in a negative float

    D.   Fast-tracking results in a negative float

4. The project LARA has activity A and activity R. Activity A is for 10 days and has an early start on day 5 and a late start on day 5. Activity A is preceded by activity R. activity R is for 15 days and has an early finish on day 30 and the late finish on day 35. Activity A:

    A.   Is on the critical path

    B.   Has a lag

C.   Is progressing well

D.   Is not on the critical path

5.   Your management asked you to reduce the overall project duration by 2 days. All the activities in the project are for 4 days. You discussed with your team ways to reduce the project duration by 2 days. Your team is in the firm view that no activity can be fast-tracked. However, they are willing to work overtime for one day of the weekend. You have only 2 team members. Which of the two activities would you allocate for overtime so that the project duration effectively can be reduced by 2 days? The project PDM is given below:

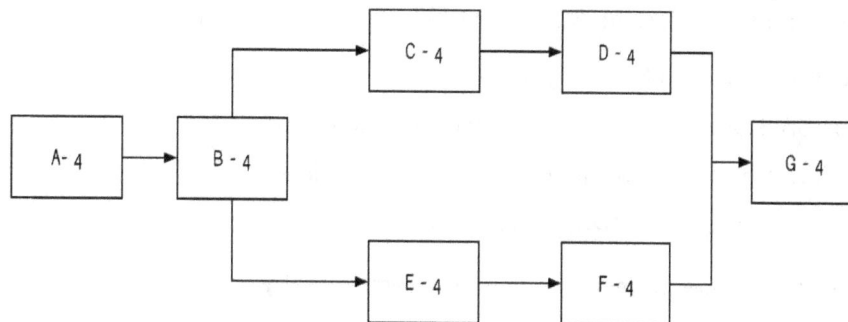

A.   C and D

B.   E and F

C.   A and F

D.   A and E

6.   TORO is a next-generation robot that is targeted to be used for household work. The robot will be able to operate dishwashers and would be able to clean the floors. Before your team starts designing the robot, the first phase is to understand the market. You have planned several workshops and surveys in sequence. Due to major floods in the region, project TORO is way behind schedule. What should be your next step to control the project schedule delay? Your management has agreed to provide all the resources needed to help control the schedule.

A.   Use a fast-tracking approach

B.   Use a crashing approach

C.   Control schedule

D.   Do resource optimization

7.   You planned phase2 to begin before phase1 completion. This can be termed as:

A.   Crashing

B.   Fast-tracking

C.   On-demand scheduling

D.   Agile scheduling

8.   Which agile project artifact can showcase the project vision, milestones, and release plans at a high level?

A.   Project schedule plan

B.   Scrum integration

C.   Product Backlog

D.   Product roadmap

9.   What is a milestone (Select the BEST answer)?

A.   Milestones are marked for payments.

B.   Milestones are regular activities with zero duration.

C.   Milestone depicts a significant point or event in a project.

D.   The schedule should always have milestones.

10.   While working with the project schedule, you realize that you cannot start one of the activities without getting the requisite approvals from the government regulatory body. What type of dependency is described in the above scenario?

A.   Mandatory- Internal dependency

B.   Mandatory- External dependency

C.   Discretionary - Internal dependency

D.   Discretionary - External dependency

11.   Identify the FALSE statement with respect to the resource calendar:

A.   A resource calendar identifies working days and shifts that are available for scheduled activities.

B.   Resource calendars specify when and how long identified project resources will be available during the project.

C.   Resource calendar information, potentially available during a planned activity period, is used for estimating resource utilization.

D.   A resource calendar is a calendar that classifies the working days and shifts for each resource.

12.   You are creating the project schedule for project XENA. Your project is on a tight schedule, and there is absolutely no float in most of the activities. One major hurdle for activity A is that it requires approval from a concerned regulatory body. You anticipate that this activity has the potential to delay the whole project. What would you do?

A. Create a project buffer to handle delays from activity A

B. Highlight the issue in the status meetings

C. Bribe the regulatory personnel in order to accelerate approvals

D. Insert a feeding buffer after the activity A, so that delay can be handled

13. You are working on a project schedule. The concern is activity Z. The team feels that in the worst-case scenario, it will take 40 days. In a best-case scenario, this activity may take 20 days, but the team is optimistic that they should be able to complete the task in 22 days. What is the expected duration for activity Z using PERT?

   A. 27 days

   B. 24 days

   C. 22 days

   D. 21 days

14. Your commute from home to the office typically takes 1.5 hours. Some days are worse, and it takes as long as 3 hours. Some lucky days you get better roads and no congestion, and the drive takes only 1 hour. What is the expected duration for the drive if you use triangular estimates?

   A. 1.4 Hours

   B. 2.15 Hours

   C. 1.5 Hours

   D. 1.8 Hours

15. Your commute from home to the office typically takes 1.5 hours. Some days are worse, and it takes as long as 3 hours. Some lucky days you get better roads and no congestion, and the drive takes only 1 hour. What is the expected duration for the drive if you use beta estimates?

   A. 1.6 Hours

   B. 2.15 Hours

   C. 1.5 Hours

   D. 1.8 Hours

16. The project ATOM has few risks. Things like resource allocation delays and approval delays may hamper the project schedule. You, as the Project Manager, inserted a buffer of 10 days to the milestone date. Which type of buffer did you use?

   A. Project buffer

   B. Feeding buffer

   C. Milestone buffer

   D. Time buffer

17. Your customer requested the project schedule to be fast-tracked to 5 days earlier than planned. When you discussed this request with all the stakeholders, it was agreed that the project would be given extra resources so that the project could be finished 5 days earlier than the planned date. You plan to put them into activities so that activity duration can be reduced to achieve the desired result. Which technique did you use to shorten the schedule?

   A. Fast tracking
   B. Crashing
   C. Resource optimization
   D. Negotiation

18. _____ tracks the work that remains to be completed in the iteration backlog.

   A. Earned value analysis
   B. Burndown chart
   C. Storyboarding
   D. Taskboards

19. The team was able to complete 6 story points in the first iteration and 10 story points in the second iteration. What would be the team's velocity for the next sprint?

   A. 6
   B. 10
   C. 8
   D. 9

20. Refer project PetZ -Burndown chart. What is the team's velocity for the sprint?

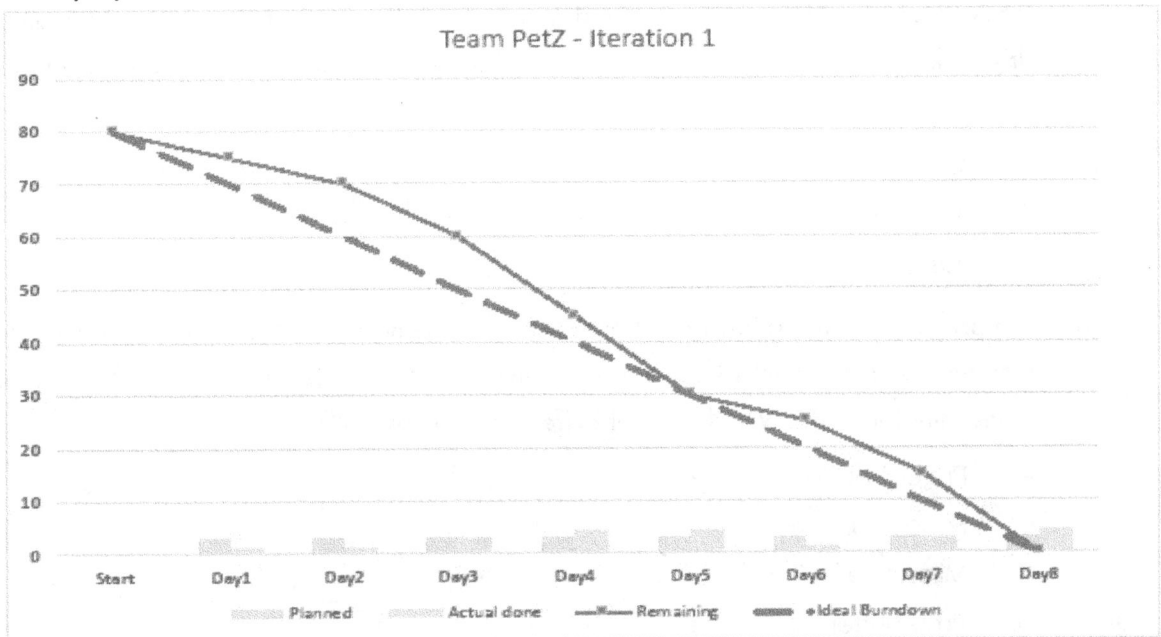

Team PetZ - Iteration 1

A.   90

B.   80

C.   70

D.   50

21.   Refer project PetZ -Burndown chart. On which day was the project on schedule?

A.   Day6

B.   Day2

C.   Day5

D.   Day7

22.   Refer project PetZ -Burndown chart. On day2, the Petz team was?

A.   Behind schedule

B.   Ahead of schedule

C.   On Schedule

D.   Can't say

23.   Refer project PetZ -Burndown chart. How many stories were yet to complete on day 5?

A.   80

B.   30

C.   50

D.   Can't say

24.   You are on an expedition in the forest with two of your friends. You have planned to do activities A, B, and C.

→   A and B can be done in parallel.

→   C needs both A and B to be completed.

→   A is for 4 days.

→   B is for 2 days, and C is for 6 days.

→   C can be divided amongst all of you equally.

How many days are required to complete all the activities?

A.   12 days

B.   10 days

C.   6 days

D.   8 days

25. You are on an expedition in the forest with two of your friends. You have planned to do activities A, B, and C. A and B can be done in parallel. C needs both A and B to be completed. A is for 4 days. B is for 2 days, and C is for 6 days. C can be divided amongst all of you equally. You and your friends completed activities A and B. However, due to unexpected rain, you had to stop. The rain continued for 2 days and resulted in no work. Calculate the total duration of the expedition.

    A.   12 days
    B.   10 days
    C.   6 days
    D.   8 days

26. You are on an expedition in the forest with two of your friends. You have planned to do activities A, B, and C. A and B can be done in parallel. C needs both A and B to be completed. A is for 4 days. B is for 2 days, and C is for 6 days. C can be divided amongst all of you equally. However, due to unexpected rain, you had to stop. The rain continued for 2 days and resulted in no work. On the third day, the rain continued, but you decided to carry out activity C. However, your team efficiency is reduced by 50%. Calculate the total duration of the expedition.

    A.   12 days
    B.   10 days
    C.   6 days
    D.   8 days

27. Refer to the diagram below. Select the correct statement about activity A and activity B:

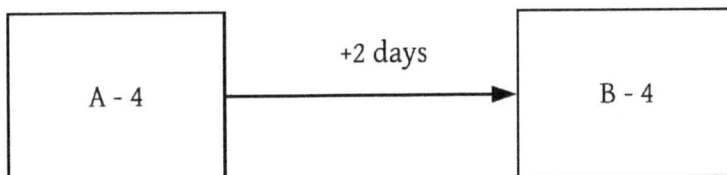

    A.   A and B have start to finish relationship and have a lag of 2 days
    B.   A and B have start to finish relationship and have a lead of 2 days
    C.   A and B have finish to start relationship and have a lag of 2 days
    D.   A and B have finish to start relationship and have a lead of 2 days

28. What would be the best way to show the milestones in the schedule?

    A.   Milestone chart

    B.   What-If analysis

    C.   PDM diagram

    D.   Critical path

29. The project ZOHO has a low-risk rating and adequate resources. All the activities have started as per the schedule. While preparing the status report, you noticed that a few of the activities are not completed as per the plan. When you checked with your team, the team responded that a few unseen issues came up and resulted in the delay. Your team assured you that they would work overtime and turn around the situation. You are fully confident of the team and of achieving the millstones. What would you write in the project report?

    A.   Project status is red as the team is behind schedule

    B.   Project status is green as the team is in full control of the schedule

    C.   Project status is yellow as the team is behind schedule, but you have a plan of action to control it

    D.   Project status is out of control, and you need to escalate and get more resources

30. Refer to the diagram below and select the correct relationship between activity A, B, and C:

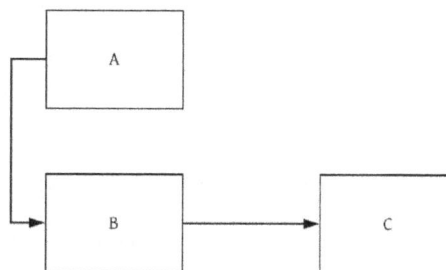

    A.   Task A and B have FF relationship, and Task B and C have SF relationship.

    B.   Task A and B have FF relationship, and Task B and C have FS relationship.

    C.   Task A and B have SS relationship, and Task B and C have SF relationship.

    D.   Task A and B have SS relationship, and Task B and C have FS relationship.

4.2.2 ANSWERS: PROCESS | SCHEDULE MANAGEMENT

Answer	Why
Answer 1 - B	This question is the BEST answer technique question. If you look at choice C, that seems reasonable. You know that resource optimization can be achieved with resource-leveling and resource smoothing. So, essentially this question is asking you to select the most accurate choice. Allocating people, the work within predefined units is resource-smoothing. What is resource leveling? Changing the allocation of resources so that a resource is available to work on the activity.
Answer 2 -A	This question type is EXTRA INFORMATION. You need to check the project information and see what stands out. <ul><li>The project seems to be going at a respectable pace (good).</li><li>People seem happy (good).</li><li>The risk rating is low (good).</li><li>Activity A has an early start date of 4 and a late start date of 2 (negative float).</li><li>Activity B has a float of 3 days (positive float).</li><li>Activity R has an early start date of 5 and a late start date of 15 (positive float).</li><li>The CPI of the project is 1.2 (good).</li><li>Most of the stakeholders seem fine with the project's progress(good).</li><li>The procurement kicked off as per the plan (on track).</li></ul> So, out of all the sentences, the one that stands out is Activity A which has a negative float, i.e., already delayed. So, crash the delayed activity to control the project.
Answer 3 - B	The float is calculated by late start minus early start, so technically B is the correct choice.
Answer 4 - A	Even if you do not draw the diagram, the data given shows that activity A is on the critical path because the float for A is zero. Activity R, on the other hand, has a float of 5 days. The arrows show that there are other activities and dependencies that are not declared in the scenario. Since no data is given for the execution, i.e., how much work has been completed, you

Answer	Why
	would not be able to answer if the activities are progressing well. What you can definitely infer is that activity A has ZERO float and hence is on a critical path.
Answer 5 - C	This requires some thinking. You have 2 days extra by virtue of your team's commitment. 2 team members for 1 day. How would you use them so that you can shorten the project by 2 days? If you put your team to work on parallel activities, then the result will not be achieved, as the overall project duration will not change due to C, E, and F dependency. You can shorten activities A and F, which will directly reduce the overall project duration.
Answer 6 - A	Since the activities planned are surveys and workshops, you cannot shorten them. What you can do is plan them in parallel and use more manpower to execute and analyze results. Control schedule is the process that is performed in the above scenario and may not be the best answer.
Answer 7 - B	Fast-tracking is performing work in parallel.
Answer 8 - D	A product roadmap is a high-level, strategic document that maps out the general stages of a product's development.
Answer 9 - C	Out of all the above choices, C is the BEST choice and hence is the answer.
Answer 10 - B	The dependency is external (Government) and is mandatory (Regulatory). So, the dependency type would be mandatory – external.
Answer 11 - A	A. A resource calendar identifies working days and shifts that are available for scheduled activities. FALSE. A project calendar is used for declaring the overall project working time B. Resource calendars specify when and how long identified project resources will be available during the project. TRUE C. Resource calendar information, potentially available during a planned activity period, is used for estimating resource utilization. TRUE D. A resource calendar is a calendar that classifies the working days and shifts for each resource. TRUE
Answer 12 - D	USE BEST ANSWER Technique: A. Create a project buffer to handle delays from activity A: Can be done; see if there is a better answer B. Highlight the issue in the status meetings: Can be done, see if there is a better answer

Answer	Why
	C. Bribe the regulatory personnel in order to accelerate approvals: No— incorrect choice
	D. Insert a feeding buffer after the activity A, so that delay can be handled: BEST answer; you will need a project buffer that can absorb delay for all the nodes, but to ensure that other activities do not suffer due to delay in one activity, it makes sense to use feeding buffers after the said activity that may be delayed.

Answer 13 - B	This is a FORMULA question. What is the formula to calculate the expected duration using Beta /PERT calculation? ED = (pessimistic duration + 4* Most Likely + optimistic)/ 6 Optimistic duration = 20, Pessimistic estimate = 40, Most likely = 22 ED = (40 + (4*22) + 20)/6 = 24.3 days. Rounding off will give 24 days.
Answer 14 - D	What is the formula to calculate expected duration using average/triangular calculation? ED = (pessimistic duration + Most Likely + optimistic)/ 3 Optimistic duration = 1, Pessimistic estimate = 3, Most likely = 1.5 ED = (1 + (1.5) + 3)/3 = 1.8 hours.
Answer 15 - A	Understand that the question has changed. Now the formula to be used is for the BETA estimate. What is the formula to calculate the expected duration using Beta /PERT calculation? ED = (pessimistic duration + 4* Most Likely + optimistic)/ 6 Optimistic duration = 1, Pessimistic estimate = 3, Most likely = 1.5 ED = (1 + (4*1.5) + 3)/6 = 1.6 hours.
Answer 16 - A	You used the critical chain technique, and the buffer type described here (before the end of the project) is the project buffer. There is nothing called a milestone buffer. Both the project buffer and feeding buffer are type project buffers and thus not the best choice.
Answer 17 - B	You crashed the activities by adding resources.

Answer	Why
Answer 18 - B	An iteration burndown chart tracks the work that remains to be completed in the iteration backlog.
Answer 19 - C	Team velocity is the average of all the sprints, i.e., (6+10)/2 = 8
Answer 20 - B	The total story points to be completed on day zero at project start is 80. This can be referred to as the team's velocity (sprint of 2 weeks, 4 days a week).
Answer 21 - C	The project was on schedule for only one day, i.e., day5. The start and end of the sprint are not accounted for (should be started and completed on schedule)
Answer 22 - A	The project was behind schedule on day2. The planned story point to complete was 20, and the actual completion was only 10.
Answer 23 - B	The team was on schedule on day 5. The total number of stories that were yet to be completed was 30 points.
Answer 24 - C	Refer to the CPM.

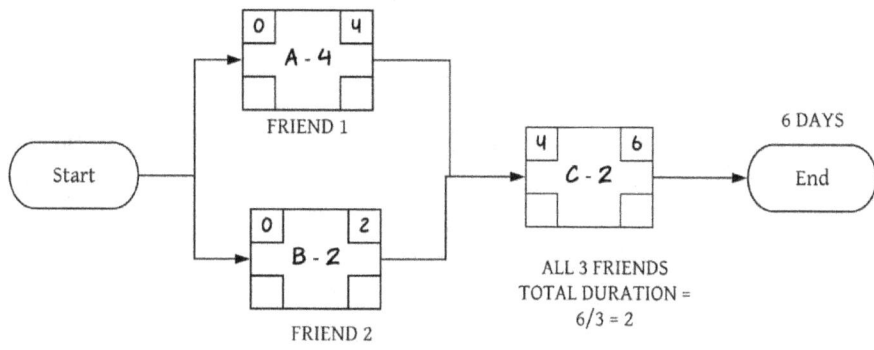

Answer 25 - D   Refer to the CPM

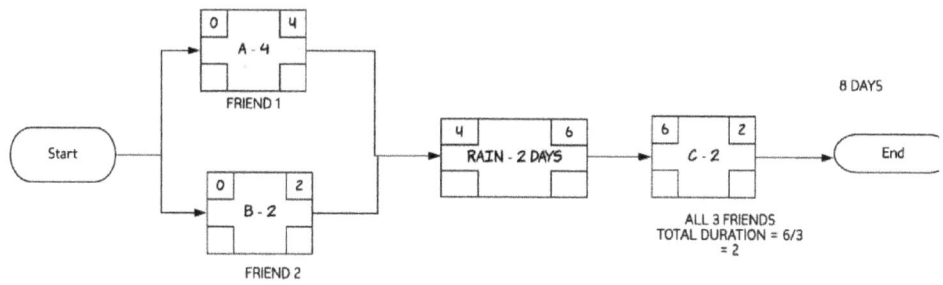

Answer	Why
Answer 26 - B	50% efficiency for the remaining task. C, if it can be completed with 100% efficiency in 2 days, now will get completed in 4 days. Now your expedition will be over in only 10 days.

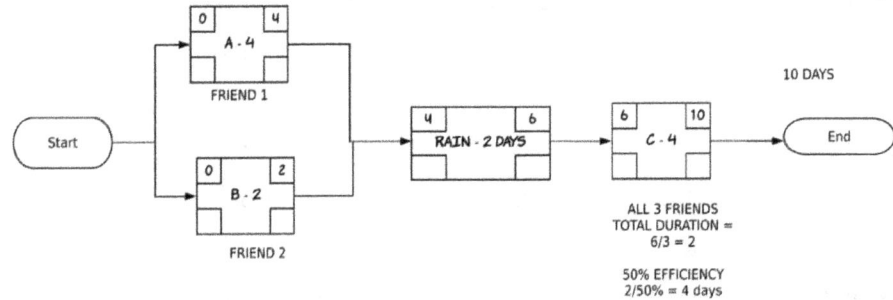

Answer 27 - C	The plus sign denotes a lag. B cannot start until A finishes. This is a finish-to-start relationship with a lag of 2 days.
Answer 28 - A	A milestone chart focuses on planned significant events scheduled to occur at specific times in the program.
Answer 29 - C	The project is delayed but under your control, and specific actions are planned. The best status color is YELLOW.
Answer 30 - D	If you have issues in understanding activity relationships, recap. A and B have SS relationship. B and C have an FS ((most used relationship).

4.3 PROCESS | COST MANAGEMENT

RECOMMENDED READINGS

PMBOK™ 6:

Chapter 7. Cost Management

Pass PMP in 21 Days I – Study Guide:

Chapter 7. Cost Management

4.3.1 QUESTIONS: PROCESS | COST MANAGEMENT

1. To create the cost estimates, you used a calculation sheet called function point analysis. A function point is a unit of measurement to express the business functionality of an information system and the cost of a single unit calculated from past projects. Your team wrote the units in corresponding columns, and the sheet calculated the overall function points. Which technique did you use to arrive at the cost estimates with this calculation sheet?

    A. Bottom-up estimates

    B. Analogous estimates

    C. Three-point estimates

    D. Parametric estimates

2. While analyzing the project status report, you calculated the metrics of SPI at 1.6 and CPI at 0.9. What would be your plan to control the project?

    A. Reduce resources to control cost

    B. Add resources to control cost

    C. Utilize contingency reserves

    D. Utilize management reserves

3. The EVM technique monitors three key dimensions for each work package and control account: Planned Value (PV), Earned Value (EV), and Actual Cost (AC). What does EV- PV denote?

    A. Cost Performance Index

    B. Cost Variance

    C. Schedule Performance Index

    D. Schedule Variance

4. You are managing a project called SPARK. The project was initiated to streamline the current telecom processes across all the client's affected countries. To achieve the desired outcome, the system needs to roll out eight components in the next 200 days. As per the plan, you should have completed 50% of the work by today, which is the 100th day. Your team is working overtime and has spent 55% of the allocated hours but has only been able to complete 40% of the work. What are the current CPI and SPI of the project?

    A. CPI is 0.73, and SPI is 0.8

    B. CPI is 73%, and SPI is 80%

    C. CPI is 0.8, and SPI is 0.73

    D. CPI is 80%, and SPI is 73%

5. The project COLA-X has an SPI of 0.9 and a CPI of 1. The BAC of the project was estimated to be $10 Million. What is the forecasted EAC if the BAC estimate was ROM?

   A. $750,000 to $1.25 Million

   B. $500,000 to $1.5 Million

   C. $950,000 to $1.1 Million

   D. $750,000 to $1.75 Million

6.   Which of the following is the best method for visually showcasing project progress (Planned vs. Actual)?

   A.   Histograms

   B.   Gantt chart

   C.   Network diagram

   D.   Milestone chart

7.   A scrum team has 8 team members having different skill sets. They are billed to the customer for their time on the project. The billing cycle is monthly. The billing was 80000 USD for this month. The scrum timebox selected by this team is 2 weeks. What is the total budget for each scrum?

   A.   USD 80000

   B.   USD 40000

   C.   USD 36360

   D.   USD 36364

8.   The project FUSION status report shows a CPI of 0.5 and SPI of 1.2, with a forecasted budget of USD 1.5 Million. What was the initial budget, assuming CPI is constant throughout the project?

   A.   1.8 Million

   B.   1.25 Million

   C.   1 Million

   D.   0.75 Million

9. The project NEO's status report shows the following information: CPI is 0.9, SPI is 1.1. What does this information convey?

   A.   The project is under control

   B.   The project has some minor deviations

   C.   The project costs are more than planned and is ahead of schedule

   D.   The project costs are more than planned and is behind schedule

10. You are preparing a status report for project MILAP. As per the project plan, you should have completed 50% of the MILAP workshops. You have 20 total workshops planned for this phase of project MILAP. You are asked by your management to revise the total efforts for the phase, keeping the delay in mind. Which EVM term would be used to convey this information?

    A. Budget at Completion

    B. Actual Costs

    C. Estimate at Completion

    D. Estimate to Complete

11. "A measure of the cost performance that must be achieved with the remaining resources in order to meet a specified management goal, expressed as the ratio of the cost to finish the outstanding work to the budget available." This is the definition of which EVM term?

    A. To Complete Performance Index (TCPI)

    B. Estimate at Completion (EAC)

    C. Budget at Completion (BAC)

    D. Cost variance (CV)

12. You work in a retail headquarters. You are put in charge of project TARGET, implementing a major customer and royalty management update on the systems. The company believes that this will outperform all current competition and is fully behind you. It is always implied that the faster you go to market with the project TARGET, the better the outcome will be. You are preparing vital stats for the project, which show an SPI of 1.3 and CPI of 0.9. Keeping the current pace of work in mind, you know that the CPI will be constant or may reduce further to 0.8. What would be your response when you asked to justify the overspending in the meeting?

    A. Inform the stakeholders that you are well within the definitive estimate range

    B. Inform the stakeholders that you are well within the ROM estimate range

    C. Ask sponsors to reduce the scope to control CPI

    D. Emphasize that the priority for the project is going live on or before the planned time and, with this pace, you are well ahead of schedule, which will give you a more competitive edge and increase income long term.

13. The project MEHAM shows following data:

    BAC = $2 Million

    AC = $1.1 Million

    PV = $1.1 Million

    EV = $800,000

The management has asked you for the total estimated project costs looking at the current spending rate. What is your response?

A. The management wants the Cost Variance which is minus $300,000

B. The management wants the Schedule Variance, which is minus $300,000

C. The management wants the Estimate at Completion, which is $1.45 Million

D. The management wants the Estimate at Completion, which is $2.75 Million

14. **You have the following data, Which month had the best CPI and SPI?**

	PV	EV	AC
Month 1	1000	900	900
Month 2	2000	2200	2100
Month 3	3000	2800	3200
Month 4	4000	3900	3800

A. Month 1

B. Month 2

C. Month 3

D. Month 4

15. **The project OLA has a TCPI of 1.3. What does this information convey?**

A. The project is under budget and is in a position to overspend

B. The project is over budget, and you need to control the costs

C. It will be easy to complete the project within the allocated budget

D. It will be difficult to complete the project within the allocated budget

16. **The project BANA has a TCPI of 1.6. What does this information convey wrt CPI of the project?**

A. CPI >1

B. CPI = 1

C. CPI <1

D. Not enough information available to calculate CPI

17. **Which estimating method tends to be the most time-consuming and precise for arriving at the cost estimate?**

A. Bottom-up estimation

B. Analogous estimation

C. Definitive estimation

D. ROM estimation

18.   Select the FALSE statement:

   A.   The cost baseline is the approved version of the time-phased project budget

   B.   Cost estimates and approved budget tend to be the same

   C.   Cost estimates and approved budget refer to two different variables

   D.   Contingency reserves are included in the cost baseline

19.   What does product life cycle cost include?

   A.   The sum of the cost of all project phases

   B.   The sum of the cost of feasibility and actual implementation of the project

   C.   The sum of all project activities costs and the contingency funds

   D.   The total sum of project and operations, and maintenance costs

20.   Project AXO-ONE was initiated last week. You were made Project Manager without your consent. Your sponsor asked you to quickly estimate the project costs and resource requirements so that the same can be initiated within the organization. You worked on the estimates by calling a workshop of the SMEs and asking their opinions on pessimistic, most likely, and optimistic estimates on project components and added a buffer to handle any unforeseen risks. The estimate you supplied would be called:

   A.   Definitive estimates, using expert judgment

   B.   ROM estimates, using expert judgment

   C.   Definitive estimates, using three-point estimates

   D.   ROM estimates, using three-point estimates

21.   What is the main difference between agile and traditional approaches regarding cost, scope, and time?

   A.   None

   B.   Agile works on the principle that changes are acceptable and welcomed

   C.   In a traditional approach, the scope is fixed, and time and cost are variables; in an agile approach, the schedule is fixed, and scope and costs are variables

   D.   In a traditional approach, the cost is fixed, and time and scope are variables; in an agile approach, the scope is fixed and time and costs are variables

22.   You are creating the project estimates for the upcoming phase (PHASE 3) of project VANILLA. The customer asked you for cost estimates so that he can provision them in the project budget. You created an excel sheet and wrote the per-hour cost based on the SME rate, as per the contract. You further added the quantities of each type of resource and multiplied them by the resource rate, as per the rate card. Which type of estimation technique did you use to arrive at the final estimates?

A. Analogous

B. Expert judgment

C. Three-point estimate

D. Parametric estimate

23. An agile team has two weeks of iteration timebox and has 8 team members. The team is working on web application development and has not decided to buy anything from outside. Select the TRUE statement:

A. Agile teams control project costs actively, and this is one of the key matrices

B. Agile teams manage project value through timebox without worrying about costs

24. You are in the early cycle of project planning. You present the cost estimates for the project to get the project funding. However, your senior management denied the request. They wanted a more accurate estimate for the project. What should you do?

A. Resign. The senior management cannot ask for better estimates, as you are only at the start of the project.

B. Politely deny the request by emphasizing that the project is at the initial stages and you can only come up with ROM estimates at this time

C. Work with your team to further decompose and estimate to prepare a basis for estimates

D. Work with the PMO to get an estimation template

25. You are managing project ROLTA for a book publishing firm. The budget is fixed. The current analysis of the project shows a CPI of 1.2 and SPI of 0.8. What should be your next step to control the project?

A. The project is ahead of schedule and over budget

B. The project is behind and under budget

C. Reduce the resources on the project so that you can control cost

D. Crash the project so that you can control the schedule

26. _____is the realized cost incurred for the work performed on an activity during a specific time period. It is the total cost incurred in accomplishing the work

A. Actual cost

B. Planned value

C. Earned value

D. Earned costs

27. _____ analyzes the project performance over time to determine whether the project performance is improving or deteriorating.

    A. Trend analysis

    B. EVM analysis

    C. Contingency analysis

    D. Risk analysis

28. Select the FALSE statement with regard to reserve analysis:

    A. Opportunities may lead to lesser reserves on the project

    B. Unused contingency reserves may be removed from the project budget

    C. Additional contingency reserves can be requested while controlling costs

    D. Opportunities may lead to added reserves on the project

29. You are made manager for a critical project, VENUS. You worked with your team and estimated all the activities and prepared a basis of estimates. You also added reserves to manage any unforeseen risks. What is the major step to achieving a cost baseline?

    A. Present the estimation to the sponsor for approval

    B. Add management reserves

    C. Add overheads to all costs

    D. Add trend analysis and get authorization

30. EVM term _____ is a measure to forecast remaining costs towards project completion.

    A. EAC

    B. ETC

    C. CPI

    D. TCPI

4.3.2 ANSWERS: PROCESS | COST MANAGEMENT

Answer	Why
Answer 1 - D	Parametric estimating is an estimating technique in which an algorithm is used to calculate cost or duration based on historical data and project parameters. The keyword for parametric estimation is calculations. The keywords for three-point estimates are optimistic, pessimistic, and most likely.
Answer 2 - A	Since you are ahead of schedule (SPI >1) and over budget, you can control costs by cutting down on your resources. The project's progress may slow down, but the spending will be controlled. Choice B is absolutely wrong. Choice C may be a valid choice if you have miscalculated or the increase in spending is due to some risks.
Answer 3 - D	EV – PV is Schedule Variance. Please remember all the EVM formulas.

Answer 4 - A

BAC	PV	EV	AC	SPI	CPI	SV	CV
200	100	80	110	0.80	0.73	-20.00	-30.00

Answer	Why
Answer 5 - D	Since the CPI is 1, the EAC and BAC are the same. For ROM estimates, the range is -25% to +75%.

25%	1000000	750000
75%	1000000	1750000

Answer	Why
Answer 6 - C	A horizontal bar chart or Gantt chart of high-level activities can be shown to show progress visually. It would be difficult to show progress using a milestone chart (you can show achieved milestones but not all progress).
Answer 7 - D	The billing was 80000 USD for 22 days (default is 22 days in a month). Scrum is for two weeks, i.e., 5 days a week. The calculation is = 80000/22*10 = 36364 USD
Answer 8 - A	The spending rate is double the planned rate, so the CPI is 0.5. To calculate the EAC with a constant CPI, the formula is EAC = BAC /CPI. Use this formula to calculate. BAC = EAC * CPI = 1.5 *0.5 = 0.75 Million
Answer 9 - C	A CPI or SPI less than 1 is not good. The project NEO's CPI is less than 1, so the project is spending more than planned. If the SPI is greater than 1, this means that the project is ahead of schedule. As such, choice C is most correct.

Answer	Why
Answer 10 - C	See the keyword TOTAL efforts, meaning all the efforts. EAT is the revised total efforts or cost.
Answer 11 - A	The To-Complete Performance Index (TCPI) is a measure of the cost performance required to meet a specified management goal with the remaining resources, expressed as the ratio of the cost to finish the outstanding work to the remaining budget.
Answer 12 - D	All the choices seem valid. However, since you, as a Project Manager, should be aware of the portfolio goals, you need to work towards achieving the required goals. The major objective for this project is to be rolled out faster to capture more profits. Choice D is the best choice to discuss and explain. If the senior management says no, then come back and release resources.
Answer 13 - D	Your management has asked you for EAC. Check the keyword TOTAL. Calculate the EAC with the formula, and you will get:

BAC	PV	EV	AC	SPI	CPI	SV	CV	EAC
20,00,000	1100000	800000	1100000	0.73	0.73	3,00,000	3,00,000	27,50,000

Answer	Why
Answer 14 - B	Month 2 seems to be better with regard to CPI and SPI.

	PV	EV	AC	SPI	CPI
Month 1	1000	900	900	0.90	1.00
Month 2	2000	2200	2100	1.10	1.05
Month 3	3000	2800	3200	0.93	0.88
Month 4	4000	3900	3800	0.98	1.03

Answer	Why
Answer 15 - B	TCPI is the required spending rate. A TCPI greater than 1 means that CPI is less than 1, which means that you need to control costs. Hence choice B is the best answer.
Answer 16 - C	TCPI is the required spending rate. A TCPI greater than 1 means that CPI is less than 1.
Answer 17 - A	A bottom-up estimation requires more time in comparison with other estimating techniques, as you need to estimate for each activity and then add the final outcome.
Answer 18 - B	This is a typical TRUE/FALSE type of question, so let's examine each choice and see if they are TRUE or FALSE: A. **The cost baseline is the approved version of the time-phased project budget - TRUE**

Answer	Why
	B. Cost estimates and approved budget tend to be the same - FALSE
	C. Cost estimates and approved budget refer to two different variables - TRUE
	D. Contingency reserves are included in the cost baseline - TRUE
	So choice B is the right answer. The estimates may be rejected by the senior management, and the approved budget can be lower than requested, or vice versa.
Answer 19 - D	Product life cycle cost is the cost of the product from inception to closure, i.e., all the costs while creating and maintaining the product, which is project + operations cost.
Answer 20 - D	This question is all about conflicting information. If you check in-depth, you will find that estimates are determined at the start, during the initiating phase. You do use SMEs, but the information is gathered with three parameters (optimistic, pessimistic, and most likely). These are called three-point estimates. So the correct answer is ROM estimates, using three-point estimates.
Answer 21 - C	The one major difference in an Agile approach is that the deliveries/iterations are of fixed duration (i.e., a one-week drop or two-week drop). The scope may change to accommodate the drop schedule, whereas, in the normal method, the scope is fixed and timelines are calculated/prepared to deliver the scope.
Answer 22 - D	A parametric estimate involves calculations.
Answer 23 - B	Understand that agile is change based methodology. For agile teams, the most important aspect is to deliver value through the timely release of the product. Statement B is a better statement for agile methodology.
Answer 24 - C	The management's request is fair. To achieve that, you need to use a bottom-up approach, so work with SMEs to decompose and estimate—choice C. Getting a template from PMO may help but is not the best choice. You still need to decompose further using the template.
Answer 25 - D	The question asks you what the next steps to control the project will be. The current state of the project is that you are behind schedule and have some money left (under budget). The next logical move would be to add more resources so that the project schedule can be controlled.

Answer	Why
Answer 26 - A	Actual cost (AC) is the realized cost incurred for the work performed on activity throughout a specific time period.
Answer 27 - A	The performance of any variable over time is called trend analysis (e.g., gold rate, share rate, etc.).
Answer 28 - A	This is a TRUE/FALSE question. Let's analyze: A. Opportunities may lead to lesser reserves on the project: FALSE; opportunities can provide money to the project B. Unused contingency reserves may be removed from the project budget: **TRUE** C. Additional contingency reserves can be requested while controlling costs: **TRUE** D. Opportunities may lead to added reserves on the project: TRUE; opportunities can provide money to the project You need to remember risk management. A risk can be a threat. The threat takes money away. Or opportunity – that can yield more money for the project and organization. The money can be resource-saving, time savings, cash, etc.
Answer 29 - A	You estimated for project cost. The next logical step is to get it baselined. You do that in the "determine budget" process. What you do here is seek management approval and get the required funding, so A is the best answer.
Answer 30 - B	The Total Cost is EAC, and the remaining cost is ETC. The question is about the remaining costs, which is Estimate to Complete.

4.4. PROCESS | QUALITY MANAGEMENT

RECOMMENDED READINGS

PMBOK™ 6:

Chapter 8. Quality Management

Pass PMP in 21 Days I – Study Guide:

Chapter 8. Deliverable Quality

4.4.1 QUESTIONS: PROCESS | QUALITY MANAGEMENT

1. You are working on a construction project called WISH TOWN. Your team is busy in construction after obtaining the necessary approvals. You have planned for testing after the construction phase. Testing will involve building strength and safety tests. This is to ensure seamless approval from safety regulators. Which testing will you plan?

    A. System testing

    B. Peer testing

    C. Acceptance testing

    D. Audits

2. _____ is keeping errors out of the process, _____ is keeping errors out from the customers.

    A. Inspection, prevention

    B. Prevention, inspection

3. Indicate which cost is NOT included in the cost of quality:

    A. Cost of resources to work on planned activities

    B. Cost of resources to work on managing quality activities

    C. Cost of resources to work on quality control activities

    D. Cost to recall the product in case of product failure

4. You work with a firm called ZOMATI. It is a startup formed to revolutionize the home delivery system from various restaurants to the end-user. Of late, there have been many issues reported by the end-users on the ZOMATI delivery mechanism. You are assigned to look at the issue and come up with possible actions to solve the problem. Which quality control tool will be most helpful to get started on this task?

    A. Control charts

    B. Scatter diagram

    C. Histograms

    D. Ishikawa

5. You are the Project Manager for project ARMSTRONG. Project ARMSTRONG was initiated to streamline the uptime and understand any early warning signs at the control center for a nuclear power plant. You need to ensure that component A is always in the range of -2.5 and -1, with a mean of -2. The reading taken on day 10 shows you the following data. What would be your inference given this data about component A?

Observation	1	2	3	4	5	6	7	8
Observation reading	-1.5	-2.4	-2.2	-1.1	0.25	-0.35	-1.35	-1.13

A.   The process is in control.

B.   The process is out of control as one of the observations lies beyond the control limit.

C.   The process is out of control because the rule of seven applies.

D.   The process is in control as these are minor deviations.

6.   **The results of a shooting exercise are shown below. How would you describe the results?**

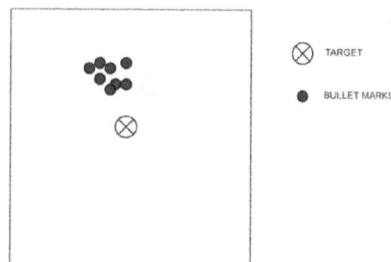

A.   Sample chart shows low precision and low accuracy.

B.   Sample chart shows high precision and high accuracy.

C.   Sample chart shows low precision and high accuracy.

D.   Sample chart shows high precision and low accuracy.

7.   **A police officer was practicing shooting as per the mandatory policy. The results of the exercise are shown below. How would you describe the results?**

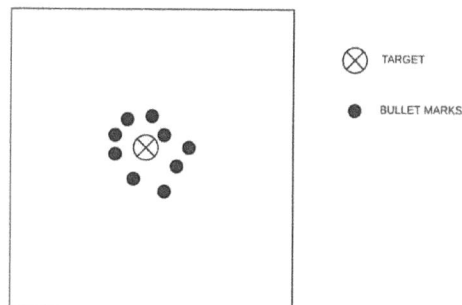

A.   Sample chart shows low precision and low accuracy.

B.   Sample chart shows high precision and high accuracy.

C.   Sample chart shows low precision and high accuracy.

D.   Sample chart shows high precision and low accuracy.

8. You are managing a project named VISTA. Your team asked you about the difference between quality and grade. What would be your response?

    A. Quality and grade are the same terms.

    B. The better the grade, the better the quality.

    C. Low grade is OK, but low quality is a problem.

    D. Low quality is OK, but low grade is a problem.

9. You are managing a book publishing project called project VENTA. The book is from a best-selling author, and you are doing everything you can to ensure that the book is error-free. After the writer submits the book content, you pass it to the copyediting process, where a qualified professional checks the book content for grammatical errors and spelling mistakes. Copyediting is a process that qualifies as:

    A. Manage quality, as you are eliminating mistakes from the book.

    B. Manage quality, as it is a preventive process.

    C. Quality control, as you are eliminating mistakes from the book.

    D. Quality control, as you are finding errors in the book.

10. A vehicle manufacturing firm recalled a few cars with a specific chassis number. The company took full responsibility for the faulty component replacement. How would you classify the cost of component replacement incurred by the car manufacturer?

    A. Prevention cost because the components were changed before they caused any issue.

    B. Appraisal cost because the firm appraised the component and then found it faulty.

    C. Internal failure cost because some specific quality processes were not followed.

    D. External failure cost because the car was recalled from the customer.

11. If your team asked you to define quality, your response would be:

    A. Quality is Plan, Do, Check, Act

    B. Quality is the degree to which a set of inherent characteristics fulfil requirements

    C. Quality is using high-grade items.

    D. Quality is high customer satisfaction.

12. Select the odd option from the given choices:

    A. Training the project team.

    B. Putting in place standards to follow.

    C. Review the deliverable before it reaches the customer.

    D. Following checklists.

13. The project BLUE is initiated to keep control of product quality. Project BLUE uses control charts as a tool to Manage Quality. While monitoring the process, a team member recorded that one of the observations was outside the control limit. What will be the next step?

    A.   Perform Pareto analysis.

    B.   Draw histogram.

    C.   Gather data to do Ishikawa analysis.

    D.   Plot scatter diagram.

14. Project JUPITER is in a testing phase. The testing team reported many errors. When you check back with the Development Team, they blame it on the testing team and their procedures. What would you do next?

    A.   Have a meeting with all stakeholders to discuss the defects in detail.

    B.   Ask the testing team to work with the Development Team and reduce the errors.

    C.   Ask the Development Team to start working on the fulfilment of errors.

    D.   Release the product for customer acceptance testing.

15. Project SIGNWAVE is getting lots of criticism from the media and stakeholders. There have been reports about the bad quality of products and questions about timelines and costs. The management is edgy and wants to get an in-depth review of the project. Which activity can help the management to start with?

    A.   Get the team to do more testing

    B.   Be a part of the daily stand-up meeting

    C.   Get audits done on the project

    D.   Ask for a detailed project report

16. Project RAKSHA was undergoing an audit. What would be the typical output of such an audit?

    A.   Change requests resulting from non-conformances

    B.   Appreciation and awards resulting from non-conformances

17. Which tool can help you to analyze and optimize a process?

    A.   Flowchart

    B.   Checklist

    C.   Histogram

    D.   Control Chart

18. _____ is the set of technical guidelines that may be applied during the design of a product for the optimization of a specific aspect.

    A.   Design of experiments
    B.   Design for X
    C.   Matrix Diagram
    D.   Nominal group technique

19. You work in a leading advertising firm. You created a task force responsible for proofreading and reviewing content before the final publication of an advertisement. The activity performed by the task force can be classified as:

    A.   Testing
    B.   Preventive action
    C.   Quality planning
    D.   Process improvement

20. You work as a Project Manager on project BETA. Project BETA is currently in the testing phase. The testing team is given instructions to follow attribute sampling. What does it mean?

    A.   The testing team will document all the attributes of any errors.
    B.   The testing team will document any errors from samples.
    C.   The testing team will document the results in Boolean (Yes/No) format from samples.
    D.   The testing team will document the results in a range of conformance from 1 to 10 from samples.

21. You found that there is an unexpected number of defects in the deliverables. That's a problem you need to solve now. What would be the typical steps to solve this problem?

    A.   Problem definition, root cause analysis, create histogram, brainstorm possible solutions, implement a solution
    B.   Problem definition, root cause analysis, possible brainstorm solutions, implement the best solution, verify the effectiveness
    C.   Root cause analysis, generate a histogram, implement 80/20 rule, verify the effectiveness
    D.   Fishbone diagram, generate a histogram, implement the 80/20 rule, verify the effectiveness

22. Check sheets are also known as:

    A.   Checklists

    B.   Matrix sheets

    C.   Sampling sheets

    D.   Tally sheets

23. Which data representation tool can show the relationship between two variables? This diagram is also known as a correlation diagram.

    A.   Ishikawa chart

    B.   Matrix chart

    C.   Scatter chart

    D.   Trend chart

24. Which data tool can help show the relationship between two variables?

    A.   Ishikawa chart

    B.   Matrix chart

    C.   Scatter chart

    D.   Trend chart

25. You are made manager of the HR program BEYOU. One of the key goals of this program is to ensure that people update time sheets regularly and every week. There are major gaps in this area even after multiple follow-ups and reminders. You hold a workshop and gather the reasons for late timesheet entry. The data which you complied is below. What would be your next step?

1	Not aware of the consequences	40%
2	Procedure not clear	39%
3	Busy with work	30%
4	Out of station	20%
5	Timesheet system down	50%
6	Supervisor advised of system being down	43%

    A.   Call the meeting of all supervisors and instruct them to ensure timely update

    B.   Create a punishment process for delay of the time sheets and advise all employees of it

    C.   Work with the systems team to monitor and correct the timesheet system uptime

    D.   Do a weekly timesheet update drill until it becomes a habit

26. You work in an event firm. The current project which you are managing is called HAPPYDAY. This project has been set up for a valued client, and your team is engaged in various events. The event kicks off with the activity of printing shirts with the company logo and a person's name. You start printing the shirts one by one, but the logo seems to be out of alignment. This is a defective shirt, so you put it in the waste bin and print another shirt. Same result. What is the activity you are performing while checking the shirt for defects in printing?

    A. Sampling under manage quality

    B. Inspection under manage quality

    C. Sampling under control quality

    D. Inspection under control quality

27. You sent the defective shirt for a quick wash so that it can be used for printing later. How would you classify the action?

    A. This was a corrective action

    B. This was a preventive action

    C. It was defect repair

    D. It was quality control

28. You attempted printing the logo on several shirts, but they all came out wrong and could not be used. You called a mechanic to look at the machine to see if it was aligned properly. The mechanic checked the machine and found it OK. However, he did a second round of printing which came out all right. Apparently, there was an issue with the way you were operating the machine. You checked the process, observing the second print carefully and noting down more details, creating a checklist which you pasted on the machine so that everyone who uses the machine will be able to print right the first time. Summarize the trigger and action.

    A. The trigger point was quality control, and action was a checklist under manage quality.

    B. The trigger point was bad printing, and action was second printing by the mechanic.

    C. The trigger point was manage quality, and action was second printing by the mechanic.

    D. The trigger point was quality control, and the action was defect repair of the shirts.

29. While printing the initial set of t-shirts, approximately 10 were misprinted. The misprinted shirts will be referred to as:

    A. Prevention cost

    B. Assessment cost

    C. Appraisal cost

    D. Waste

30. The time which you spent on creating the checklist can be referred to as:

    A. Prevention cost

    B. Assessment cost

    C. Appraisal cost

    D. Waste

4.4.2 ANSWERS: PROCESS | QUALITY MANAGEMENT

Answer	Why
Answer 1 - A	This is to set you thinking about the type of testing. Testing the entire product for overall fitment is system testing.
Answer 2 - B	Prevention (keeping errors out of the process) and inspection (keeping errors out of the hands of the customer)
Answer 3 - A	The cost of resources to work on the planned activities is not part of quality activities. Quality activities are training, Testing, process improvement, etc.
Answer 4 - D	A problem is given to you to solve. The first thing to do is qualify or define the problem statement. The next thing then would be to understand the WHY of the problem. Why this problem is happening can be determined by using a root cause or Ishikawa diagram.
Answer 5 - B	
Answer 6 - D	Precision is a measure of exactness, and accuracy is an assessment of correctness. In the sample, the dots are precise—concentrated at one spot. However, the points are far away from the center, which means less accurate
Answer 7 - C	Precision is a measure of exactness, and accuracy is an assessment of correctness. In the sample, the dots are not precise. They are scattered but near the target (i.e., more accurate).
Answer 8 - C	Low grade is OK, but low quality is a problem. Grade is the technical specifications of artifacts/items

Answer	Why
	Quality is Fit to use and as per customer requirements. Low quality is an issue.
Answer 9 - D	The process of quality control is to find errors from the finished deliverables before a customer can find them. The copyediting process is also about finding the defects so that the author can address them, and this falls under control quality.
Answer 10 - D	This is an example of external failure cost, as the deliverable was with the customer and the cost to replace the component was due to the non-conformance of quality.
Answer 11 - B	All the definitions given as choices are correct. However, stick to the PMBOK definition, which is: The degree to which a set of inherent characteristics fulfil the project requirements
Answer 12 - C	Choice A, B, and D prevent errors from happening. Testing is the only activity that assesses the deliverable and checks for errors.
Answer 13 - C	If the process is out of control, the best thing to do is to carry out a root cause analysis. One of the tools for performing a root cause analysis is the Ishikawa diagram. Histogram (Choice B) can happen only after determining root causes. Choice D—the scatter diagram—may not help you here.
Answer 14 - A	Rule of thumb – Always select interactive communication. Only A is a meeting rest of the other choices are directing. Best is to meet with the teams.
Answer 15 - C	An independent audit can help the management to get an insight into the problems. A review meeting focusing on the deliverables and project issues can be initiated once the audit results are declared by an independent internal auditor.
Answer 16 - A	An audit takes place via the manage quality process. An audit would result into non-conformances. To close, you need to either update the process or change the plan.
Answer 17 - A	A flowchart can be used to draw and analyze the process for further optimization.
Answer 18 - B	Design for X is the set of technical guidelines that may be applied during the design of a product for the optimization of a specific aspect.

Answer	Why
Answer 19 - A	Preventive action may seem like the correct answer; however, the preventive activity would eliminate the root cause and eradicate the defect from manifesting. Here in this scenario, The result is an error sheet, so it is correction/control that is being done. Correction/control is a vital part of testing.
Answer 20 - C	Attribute sampling is a YES or No answer for the sample, whereas variable sampling is a range.
Answer 21 - B	Choice B is most correct. That is - Problem definition, root cause analysis, possible brainstorm solutions, implement the best solution, verify the effectiveness

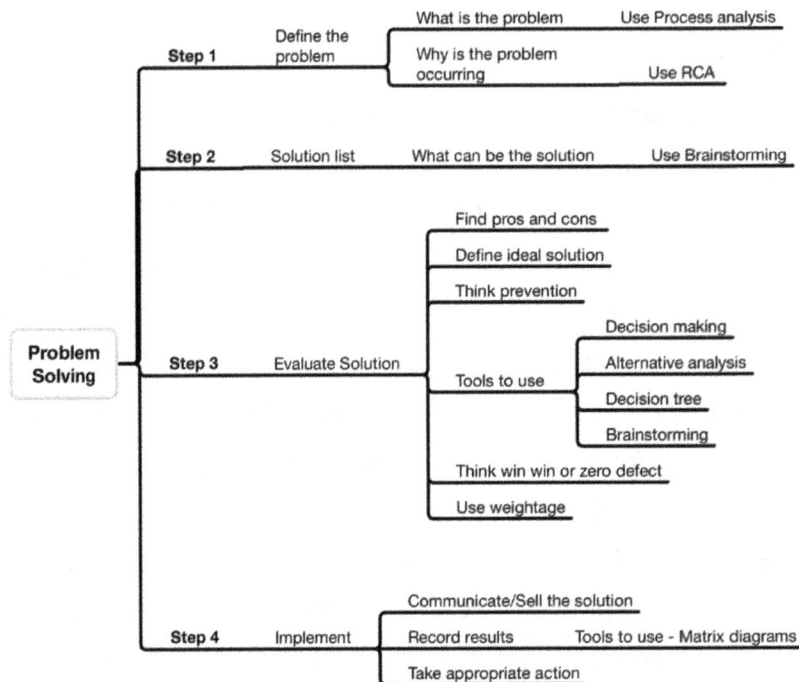

Answer 22 - D	Check sheets are also known as tally sheets. Check sheets are useful for gathering data while performing inspections.
Answer 23 - C	Two variables can be plotted on a scatter diagram to show the relationship between the variables.
Answer 24 - C	A correlation chart can be plotted to check the relationship between two variables. A scatter plot, scatter graph, and correlation chart is other names for a scatter diagram. We draw this graph with two

Answer	Why
	variables. The first variable is independent, and the second variable depends on the first. This diagram is used to find the correlation between these two variables and how they are related.
Answer 25 - C	Using the 80/20 rule, solve the biggest problem first. Checking the data, 50% of the people are unable to update the time sheets due to system unavailability. The best thing is to work with the systems team to monitor and correct the uptime.
Answer 26 - D	You are checking all the shirts, so it's not sampling. Checking the finished deliverables for defects is part of control quality. Choice D is most correct.
Answer 27 - C	Defect repair is the process of fixing the defective part or replacing it as needed. Fixing the non-conforming product (e.g., mending a shirt for later use) is defect repair.
Answer 28 - A	This one is more to educate you. The trigger for the problems was bad printing, which occurred in the process control quality. The action that you took was to inspect the process and create a checklist to prevent such occurrences. The action falls under manage quality.
Answer 29 - D	The shirts that cannot be used as a finished product will fall under waste.
Answer 30 - A	The time to create a checklist is time being spent on preventing future errors—part of the prevention cost.

4.5 PROCESS | RISK MANAGEMENT

RECOMMENDED READINGS

PMBOK™ 6:

Chapter 11. Risk Management

Pass PMP in 21 Days I – Study Guide:

Chapter 10. Risks

4.5.1 QUESTIONS: PROCESS | RISK MANAGEMENT

1. Project ALFA needs an investment of 10 million. It has a 60% chance of positive return, amounting to 110% profits, and a 40% chance of negative return amounting to a loss of all the money invested. Project BETA needs an investment of 10 million, has a 40% chance of positive return amounting to 120% profits, and a 60% chance of loss of all investment. Which project would you select?

    A. Project A because Expected Monetary Value is least negative.

    B. Project B because Expected Monetary Value is least negative.

    C. Project A because Expected Monetary Value is more positive.

    D. Project B because Expected Monetary Value is more positive.

2. Identify the risk from the below options:

    A. As per the current status report, the project is delayed

    B. The project is understaffed

    C. There may be a change in the currency conversion leading to losses while billing

    D. The last bill was not raised on time

3. What is the least correct statement about an issue:

    A. A positive project risk that has occurred is considered an issue.

    B. Issues can arise while managing the project team.

    C. An issue log is used for monitoring members responsible for resolving the specific issues by a target date.

    D. A negative project risk that has occurred is considered an issue.

4. David took over the project WELLNESS from Steve in phase2. Project WELLNESS is on-schedule, and the spending rate is within budget. People's morale was high, and client feedback was within acceptable limits. David, while going through all the documentation, could not find anything related to a risk register. What's your advice for David?

    A. Create a risk management plan and follow the plan

    B. Identify risks and mitigate all the risks

    C. Go with the flow. The project seems to be doing fine.

    D. Start monitoring the issues and risks

5. You are managing the project NINJA-X. The project seems to be under control. There were some schedule delays, but you had enough time buffer built into the project schedule. Suddenly at one of the team meetings, an urgent and major issue on data integration comes up. This issue is a major one and can derail the entire project. What is the best thing to do?

    A. Add this risk to the risk register and brainstorm for the response

    B. Set up an urgent meeting with subject matter experts to handle this issue

    C. Set up an urgent meeting with team members to understand why this issue was not forecast as a risk

    D. Update the risk event register

6. The project MEGA-M is a major initiative that will change the way policies are created and adhered to. There are many modules and touchpoints. Different teams are working on each module since the functionalities are independent, but all the modules need to work together as one working unit. Each team has more than 10 team members, and all are handling 5 parallel functionalities. What would be the major concern for you as the Project Manager for the project MEGA-M?

    A. Scope creep and integrated functionality

    B. Getting customer sign off

    C. Project schedule planning and adherence

    D. Project risk identification and planning

7. The project TEENSAFE was launched by a government department. The department is hierarchical in nature. You have a feeling that if you do focus groups to find out more details on the functionalities and risks associated with the project, you will not make much headway. So, you have decided to reach out to all the stakeholders using private surveys. Which technique did you use to collect this information?

    A. Information gathering technique

    B. Push technique

    C. Delphi technique

    D. Pull technique

8. A spare tire is carried in a motor vehicle as a replacement for one that goes flat, a blowout, or other emergencies. The spare tire is generally a misnomer, as almost all vehicles carry an entire wheel with a tire mounted on it as a spare rather than just a tire, as fitting a tire to a wheel would require a motorist to carry additional, specialized equipment. Providing a spare tire falls under which risk response strategy:

    A. Accept

    B. Mitigate

C. Transfer

D. Avoid

9. Buying extended support for your iPhone is a risk response strategy. If anything goes wrong with the phone, then the costs are covered. Which risk response strategy is used by you in buying the extended support?

A. Accept

B. Avoid

C. Transfer

D. Mitigate

10. The project EARL is a very critical project. Your team is racing against the clock, and the emphasis to meet published milestones is immense. To ensure that you meet the published milestones, you used the critical chain technique. What is the result of using the critical change technique on Project EARL?

A. The project milestone will change. You need to baseline the new schedule.

B. The schedule will have a project and feeding buffer to handle any known schedule risks.

C. The resource plan will have backup resources to handle any risks due to resources.

D. You will add management reserves to the overall project budget.

11. Risk triggers are:

A. Risk triggers are events that indicate that risk has occurred.

B. Risk triggers are events or conditions that indicate that a risk is about to occur.

12. You are managing the project 3G-AFRICA. Most of the work is outsourced, and you have planned regular checkpoints with sellers. One of the seller's performances was below acceptable limits in the last phase. While planning for the current phase, a risk to the seller's performance was identified. This risk may lead to a major impact on the project and additionally on the company's brand. You proposed to replace the seller with a new one. As a next step, the procurement team floated an RFP for the required work. You finally replaced the nonperforming seller with a new vendor. Surprisingly, the new vendor came at a lower cost too. The above risk response technique can be classified as:

A. Enhance

B. Contingent Response Strategy

C. Mitigate

D. Exploit

13. Identify the odd one out:

   A.   Risk owners and assigned responsibilities

   B.   Change requests

   C.   Agreed-upon response strategies

   D.   Contingency reserves

14. You are managing the project IGLOO. To find the maximum risk possible, you call for a meeting with your team members. Later, you also discussed business risks with a sponsor. What is the best method to find maximum risks on the project in a structured manner?

   A.   Doing brainstorming more often

   B.   By using a risk breakdown structure

   C.   By using a work breakdown structure

   D.   By doing thorough document reviews

15. You have delivered all deliverables and received sign-off from the customer. Procurements are closed. What's left is handover and project document archival. In order to do that, you start to update the risk register. How many active risks can be found in the project risk register at the time of project closure?

   A.   At least 5

   B.   1-5

   C.   Depends on the project and risks status.

   D.   Zero

16. A risk is identified in one of the work packages of the project KARMA. This work package cannot be outsourced, and there is no alternate way of doing it. The risk, if it occurs, could impact the project in an adverse manner, but it falls within the management tolerance limits. What is the best method to treat this risk?

   A.   Avoid, find out alternate ways of achieving the required result

   B.   Transfer, outsource the work to a 3rd party

   C.   Share, outsource the work to a 3rd party

   D.   Accept, do nothing

17. A new project MAX-DEL was to mobilize a team of health associates for emergency operation outsourcing for the hospital APOLLO. One of the key risks is to get the required associates in time. You have 50% of the manpower available. There is a scarcity of resources, and the hiring process is long. Which risk response strategy would you select:

   A.   Suggest management call off the project as it's not possible to mobilize a full team

   B.   Start hiring now so that you have a team in place before the mobilization date

C.   Pray to God that everything falls in place and start planning for the project

D.   Start hiring with detailed follow-ups with the hiring team. At the same time, start shortlisting contractors in case the need arises.

18.   Sarah, while creating the schedule for project MANTRA, added a project buffer in the overall schedule. Adding the project buffer to the schedule will be considered _____ risk response strategy.

A.   Avoid

B.   Exploit

C.   Mitigate

D.   Accept

19.   Mark has finished identifying the risks on the project AXE. While considering risk impact and probability, one of the risks seems to be of low impact and low probability. However, the overall urgency was high. As a policy, all the high urgency risks must be addressed. A risk response of mitigate was selected for the risk. What is the outcome of the risk after treating it with a risk mitigate response?

A.   The risk probability has reduced to zero

B.   The treatment will leave residual risk

C.   The treatment will leave a secondary risk

D.   The treatment will eliminate the risk

20.   The _____ risk response can be used for both negative and positive risks.

A.   Avoid

B.   Share

C.   Transfer

D.   Accept

21.   While discussing the project AXE with the senior manager, Linda, the customer remarked: We are OK with 10% cost variations in the budget, but no alternatives will be approved for the project go-live date. What does this statement reflect?

A.   The risk threshold for project cost is 10%

B.   The project has a risk appetite of 10%

C.   The risk threshold for the schedule is 10%, and the risk threshold for cost is 0%.

D.   The risk threshold for cost variation is 10%, and the risk threshold for schedule delay is 0%

22. While doing the analysis of cost forecasts and simulations for the project NI, you received below chart. What is the probability that the project will finish under 90 million?

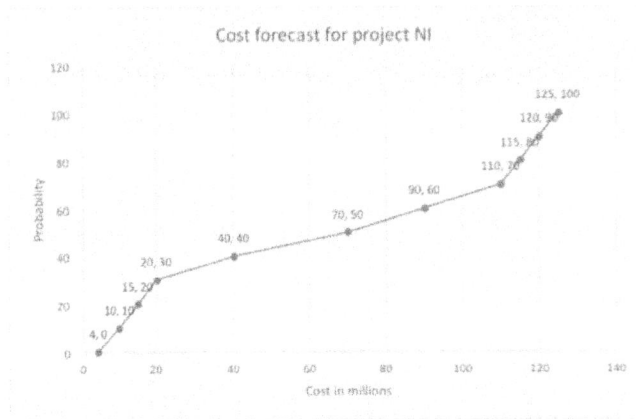

A. 50%

B. 80%

C. 60%

D. 70%

23. Referring to the cost forecast for project NI, how much is forecast as being necessary for the project to have 100% confidence?

A. 125 million

B. 120 million

C. 115 million

D. 150 million

24. Identify the diagram shown below:

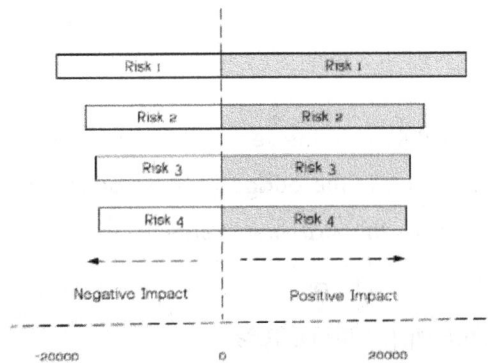

A. Tornado chart

B. Bar chart

C. Scatter chart

D. Radar chart

25. Team productivity is lower than anticipated for the project MANGOv2. How would you qualify the above statement?

    A. The project estimates were wrong and should have been estimated more carefully

    B. The project estimates should be revisited again, and a new baseline created

    C. Lower productivity should have been part of the project risks so it could be addressed using contingency reserves

    D. Lower productivity should have been part of the project risks so it could be addressed using management reserves

26. The project team for the project LEAF was in the process of identifying project risks. The manager, Sean, proposed to go in a round-robin fashion and ask each team member to present two risks that they anticipate for the project or their task. Which technique was used by Sean?

    A. Brainstorming

    B. Nominal group technique

    C. Delphi

    D. Interviews

27. A few team members were hesitant to speak up because they feared that if they started speaking of negative outcomes, they would be looked at in a negative way. To overcome this, Sean asked the team to write their comments on a yellow sticky note without mentioning their name and put the ideas/risks in the risk drop box. Which technique did Sean use to gather risks from the team?

    A. Brainstorming

    B. Nominal group technique

    C. Delphi

    D. Interviews

28. The project team LEAF identified many risks and is now in the process of allocating a priority to all of them. Each team member felt that the risk identified by them was the most important risk and needed to be prioritized. This has led to major discussions and conflicts. What would you suggest for team LEAF to avoid the situation?

    A. Use voting to arrive at the risk rating

    B. Establish risk probability and impact scale

    C. Use nominal group technique

    D. Let Sean, the manager, make a call on risk rating

29. Sean, the manager, still has a feeling that a few risks are not clearly identified. What can Sean do to identify the maximum risk on the project using a structured methodology?

    A. Use brainstorming with multiple parties

    B. Work with prompt list derived from RBS

    C. Ask an expert

    D. Check with PMO

30. One of the risks that team LEAF identified was the use of new technology. The customer demanded that a specific technology be used. The team LEAF is new to it and feels that the adoption of the new technology may hamper the project schedule. Moreover, few team members may quit due to management's expectation that they learn the new technology. Find the risk mentioned in the above scenario and how you would respond to it?

    A. New technology leading to an inefficient team. The response: Training can be given to team members. The response type is Mitigate.

    B. New technology leading to delay in the schedule. The response: Add a buffer in the project schedule. The response type is Mitigate.

    C. New technology leading to team attrition. The response: hire backup resources. The response type is Avoid.

    D. New technology leading to project delay and team attrition. The response: Training and rewards for people who get certified. The response type is Enhance.

4.5.2 ANSWERS: PROCESS | RISK MANAGEMENT

Answer	Why
Answer 1 - A	By simply looking at the percentage of returns, it feels like project B is better because the returns are high. However, when the EMV calculations are done, the picture is entirely different. Our minds tend not to look at losses.

	Initial Investment	Chance	Returns	Net Path value	Overall Value
Project ALFA	100	60%	110	10	-34
		40%	0	-100	
Project BETA	100	40%	120	20	-52
		60%	0	-100	

Answer	Why
Answer 2 - C	Risks have probability and are future events. The rest of the other options are issues that the project team must work with using workarounds.
Answer 3 - A	A positive project risk that has occurred is considered an opportunity and not an issue.
Answer 4 - A	Understand that the project is a unique work that the team is doing for the FIRST time. This is the reason it requires lots of planning. Since we are executing something new for the first time, lots of unseen issues can arise. To avoid them, the project team needs to be more diligent, watching for the unknown, and that is where risk management is crucial. So, even if the project seems to be in control right now, anything can (and often does) happen. Risk planning is very important and should be carried out the moment you take over a project. As such, choice A is most correct.
Answer 5 - B	Check the scenario again. An issue has arisen amidst the project. It was not identified as a risk earlier, so there is no response identified. Yes, you may need to add this issue as a future risk, if applicable, under the risk section along with a risk event with the current date along with the

Answer	Why
	response. However, as of now, it's an unidentified major risk that needs to be dealt with. The first thing you need to do is to attend to this issue and ensure that it is closed. This is an unplanned action, and you may need to put some heads together to deal with it. This type of response is called a workaround. Choice B is most correct. All the other things mentioned may be applied later, but not at this time.
Answer 6 - D	Many integration points, many team members, and major projects. The above keywords point toward project complexity and, in turn, towards the importance of identifying risks and managing those risks. Scope creep can also be a risk, along with customer sign-off and delay in the project schedule. The first major thing for any complex project is to ensure that you identify risks and plan for them.
Answer 7 - C	The answer could be either A (information gathering technique) or C (Delphi technique). The communication could be identified as push communication, but that's not the question. The question is how you collected the data on risks. Delphi is much more appropriate and hence is the correct choice.
Answer 8 - B	How many tires does your car have? Four. What if two tires get punctured? You are not fully covered on the risks. Or in other words, the risks still exist, and these are known as residual risks. By providing a spare tire, you have lowered the risk to an acceptable limit. This is a mitigate response.
Answer 9 - C	Buying insurance or extended support is risk transference. You cover the project/item for the risks by shifting the impact of a threat to a third party, together with ownership of the response.
Answer 10 - B	Using critical chain will result in adding buffers (project buffers and feeding buffers) to the project schedule. However, it has been mentioned that you cannot change the agreed-on milestone dates, so now you may need to analyze the schedule to ensure that you have enough buffers to handle the project delays if any come up. So, all other things being equal, option B is most correct, though the other options may also be added to achieve the required results.
Answer 11 - B	Risk triggers are events or conditions that indicate that a risk is about to occur.

Answer	Why
Answer 12 - D	A risk has a probability. The seller not performing as required has a higher probability based on past performance. As a next step, you changed the supplier. That is, you made a decision that reduces the risk of current supplier performance to ZERO. This is the "avoid" technique. Now note that you made money or saved money for the project by using this decision. That means you used/changed the risk to an opportunity. This response has no changes to exploit.
Answer 13 - B	Choices A, C, and D belong to risk management, whereas choice B is more about change management and hence is the right choice.
Answer 14 - B	A risk breakdown structure, also called a prompt list, can be used to identify risks in a structured manner. This will give a head start to the team by using pre-defined risk categories and allowing for all risks associated with a specific category to be identified while brainstorming with the team.
Answer 15 - D	See that the project is successfully closed. That means that there is no risk of baseline shifts. You might have some risks surrounding payments, closure, or operations, but those do not represent a major project risk since all the project deliverables have been successfully closed.
Answer 16 - D	The work package cannot be outsourced, so choices B and C are not valid options. There is no acceptable way to achieve the results, so choice A, avoid, is also out the window. The only valid choice left is "accept"—choice D.
Answer 17 - D	Using elimination: Choice A and C are not valid choices. Choice B seems good, but what if the resources don't get lined up per the requirements? Choice D is the best choice, as it offers a backup plan.
Answer 18 - C	Adding a project buffer reduces the probability of delays on the project but does not eliminate it, so it's not Avoid. It's "Mitigate" because you reduce the probability/impact of delay in the project to acceptable limits.
Answer 19 - B	If mitigate is being used as the risk response strategy, the risk is reduced to acceptable limits by reducing the risk probability and/or risk impact. The remaining risk is called residual risk. Choice B is most correct.
Answer 20 - D	Accept is a response strategy that can be applied to both positive and negative risks.

Answer	Why
Answer 21 - A	The risk threshold for cost is 10% for project AXE, as stated by the customer.
Answer 22 - C	Check the graph. The probability of finishing within 90 million is 60%.
Answer 23 - A	There is 100 % confidence or probability that the project will finish at the cost of 125 Million.
Answer 24 - A	The diagram shown is a tornado diagram. A tornado diagram shows or represents the data to showcase the sensitivity of the project of various elements. The highest sensitivity is placed at the top. This forms the shape of a tornado and hence is called a tornado diagram.
Answer 25 - C	A is more of a generic statement, and B can be a response. However, D is wrong. Out of all the choices, C is the best one. Typically, we know that estimates are never accurate, and for this reason, we put in some reserves when estimating. These reserves are the contingency reserves to handle any delay or any risk if estimates are wrong. C is the best answer.
Answer 26 - A	This is a typical brainstorming session described in the scenario.
Answer 27 - C	Gathering data to get unbiased and or anonymous information is the Delphi technique.
Answer 28 - B	Every person is different and can have different thought processes. This can lead to differences of opinion while discussing risk impact or probability and hence the risk rating. It's a good idea to develop a probability and impact scale to identify the correct probability level or impact of the risk to give objectivity to the discussion.
Answer 29 - B	A prompt list will help the team to identify risks from all the probable categories. Sometimes while brainstorming for risks, the team may consider only a few of the categories and might not be able to cover the breadth of the risks.
Answer 30 - D	This is a classic case of changing a negative risk to a positive risk. Using rewards and training will lead to a much more efficient and motivated team.

4.6 PROCESS | PROCUREMENT MANAGEMENT

RECOMMENDED READINGS

PMBOK™ 6:

Chapter 12. Procurement Management

Pass PMP in 21 Days I – Study Guide:

Chapter 9. procurements

4.6.1 QUESTIONS: PROCESS | PROCUREMENT MANAGEMENT

1. The Project Manager, Joe, plans to outsource some work from the project LUTO. The purchasing manager Ray, who works along with Joe for any facilitation of project purchases, wants the outsourcing to be favorable to the project costs. The outsourcing statement of work is fully developed by Joe's team. Which contract type should Ray select for outsourcing this work package?

   A. Fixed price contract

   B. Rate contract

   C. Time and Material contract

   D. Cost-plus contract

2. Adam manages the project LISA. The project is process outsourcing and requires a few domain experts for a small period while the process redesigning specifications are getting developed. Adam inquired with the PMO and functional managers, and they had no such resources in the entire organization. What would you advise Adam to do moving forward?

   A. Outsource the complete specification development phase

   B. Issue a hiring note to the hiring manager to get full-time domain experts for the project

   C. Get domain expert consultants on contract for a specific period as required by the project

   D. Ask the customer to supply the domain experts on the project

3. Which type of contract has special provisions to allow changes in the final contract price due to changed conditions, such as inflation or cost increases or decreases?

   A. Cost plus with incentives fee contracts

   B. Fixed price with economic price adjustments

   C. Fixed Price with incentive fee contracts

   D. Time and material contracts

4. Select the contract type described: "The seller is reimbursed for all allowable costs for performing the contract work and receives a predetermined incentive fee based upon achieving certain performance objectives as set forth in the contract."

   A. Fixed Price Incentive Fee Contracts

   B. Cost Plus Incentive Fee Contracts

   C. Cost Plus Award Fee Contracts

   D. Time and Material Contracts

5. Lisa is managing the project IOTA. The goal of project IOTA is to create a recreational center for the community which can serve 1,000 people from nearby localities. Lisa discussed all the work items with the team for further planning, and it was noticed that one work package lies beyond the capabilities of the project team. Further, this work package was marked as the most important item per requirement traceability matrices. It was very clear that there was little or no capability within the project team to deliver it. What is the first thing Lisa should do?

   A.   Lisa should analyze the work package with the team to arrive at a make or buy decision

   B.   Lisa should float an RFP to invite the proposals for the work package

   C.   Lisa should check with the procurement team to understand the type of contracts available

   D.   Lisa and the team should prepare the bid documents

6. Nick was in the process of evaluating the proposals that were submitted in response to the RFP REBUILD. There were a few clarification requests from sellers on some of the RFP items. What should Nick do to address the clarification requests raised by sellers?

   A.   Nick should respond to them individually

   B.   Nick should call for a pre-bid meeting with all the sellers

   C.   Nick should call for meetings with all the sellers individually

   D.   Nick should wait till the proposals are submitted

7. For industrial or commercial construction, project delivery methods are: (Select 2)

   ☐   A. Design Build Operate

   ☐   B. Design Operate

   ☐   C. Build Own Operate Transfer

   ☐   D. Design Bid

8. Incentives and awards may be used to align the objectives of buyer and seller:

   A.   FALSE

   B.   TRUE

9. The phrase terms of reference (TOR) is sometimes used when contracting for services. TOR typically includes

   A.   Tasks details of the contractor team

   B.   Standards, the contractor, to fulfil

   C.   Test plans and test cases

   D.   Change management plan for buyer organization

10. The project ALFA2 has seller selection criteria as 40% weightage on cost and 60% weightage on technical capabilities. You received a few responses to the RFP. Your team analyzed the responses and created a selection matrix. The evaluation for all the RFP responses is detailed below. Which seller would you recommend for outsourcing?

	Technical Evaluation	Project Bid
Seller A	6	4.1
Seller B	4	4.2
Seller C	3	4.3
Seller D	6	4.5

   A. Seller A

   B. Seller B

   C. Seller C

   D. Seller D

11. Evan is managing the project MATRIX. One of the work packages was marked for outsourcing as per industry standards. This will save cost, and you can focus on the core work of the project. The specifications on this work package were very crude, and not much detailing was achieved. Moreover, the work is to be performed in high-risk environments. Which contract type would you suggest for this work package outsourcing?

   A. Time and material

   B. Cost plus

   C. Fixed-price

   D. Undecided, need more information

12. You are working as the bid response manager in the seller organization. Which contract type would you favor to get maximum benefit for your organization and the least risk on the contract?

   A. Fixed Price with Economic Price Adjustment Contracts

   B. Fixed Price Incentive Fee Contracts

   C. Cost Plus Incentive Fee Contracts

   D. Cost Plus Award Fee Contracts

13. You are managing project NYSA. The project has outsourced some of the identified work. While compiling a payment request from the seller, you noticed some discrepancies. As a next step, you called the seller and informed them that you would not be paying for the submitted claim. The seller, on the other hand, insisted on the payment, giving their reasons. Since none

of you reached an agreement, you marked the expense as a dispute. Which entity is responsible for settling the disputes?

A.   Third-party organization

B.   Seller organization

C.   Buyer organization

D.   The project team

14.   Matt is trying to find the rates of some resources as per the project resource needs. Matt inquired from procurement and the PMO if either has the latest rates. He received the latest item rate list from the PMO. Matt ordered 10 specific items through the procurement manager and paid the price as per the finalized list from the project budget. Which type of procurement took place?

A.   It was a fixed price procurement

B.   It was a time and material procurement

C.   It was cost-plus procurement

D.   It was fixed price with EPA procurement

15.   What is the sole source procurement technique?

A.   When the buyer selects only one seller for procurements

B.   When only one seller responds

C.   When only one item is bought

D.   When a specific seller is asked for the proposal

16.   Select the odd one out:

A.   Request for information

B.   Request for quotation

C.   Request for proposals

D.   Pre-bid meetings

17.   You are in discussion with the procurement manager for the contract types to be selected for potential work packages. Where would you list the contract type to be selected for the project procurements:

A.   Procurement management plan

B.   Procurement strategy

C.   Bid documents

D.   Statement of work

18. You are inspecting the final deliverables provided by the seller. Once satisfied, you ask the seller to provide you with all the documentation and handover of the deliverables. You also ask the procurement team to settle all the claims by the seller as the work is complete. Which process is performed by you while closing the procurements?

    A. Planning procurements

    B. Close project or phase

    C. Make or buy process

    D. Control procurements

19. Mike is planning to outsource a few of the work packages of project ZEN. The statement of work for the work package is clear and fully developed. The work packages are many, and Mike may need several contractors. Mike is worried about the seller's priorities and wants them to be aligned with project ZEN. Which contract type would you suggest to Mike?

    A. Fixed price with EPA

    B. Cost plus with incentive fees

    C. Fixed price with incentive fees

    D. Cost plus award fee

20. Mia is managing project MARS. MARS has some requirements which can only be fulfilled by outsourcing partners. The RFP was floated, proposals were received, and Team MARS is evaluating seller proposals. The selection criteria listed in the project procurement documents is the highest technical score. Mia received the following data from the proposal evaluation team. Which seller would you recommend as per the project criteria?

	Technical Evaluation	Bid Amount
Seller A	6	5
Seller B	4	4.2
Seller C	3	3
Seller D	5.5	4.5

    A. Seller A

    B. Seller B

    C. Seller C

    D. Seller D

21. James is the Project Manager for the project METRO-D. The project METRO-D is a construction project and requires a purchasing strategy along with coordinated procurement and project activities. James wants to minimize the risk of cost and delay for all the outsourced work. What would you advise James to do?

    A. Select a fixed price contract and ensure that procurement milestones are planned and monitored, keeping the delay time in mind

    B. Select a fixed price contract and ensure that the procurement phase has some buffer to handle any delay

    C. Select a cost-plus contract and ensure that procurement milestones are planned and monitored, keeping the delay time in mind

    D. Select a cost-plus contract and ensure that the procurement phase has some buffer to handle any delay

22. Which document would be updated to mention the selected/preferred contact type for the project and procurement activities, like when to raise the procurement demand and when to receive the required items from sellers?

    A. Contract type to be used to be mentioned in the procurement management plan and procurement activities in the bid document

    B. Contract type to be used to be mentioned in the procurement strategy and procurement activities in the project schedule

    C. Contract type to be used to be mentioned in the procurement strategy and procurement activities in the bid document

    D. Contract type to be used to be mentioned in the procurement management plan and procurement activities in the procurement statement of work

23. James, while in discussion with the project team, came to one contested resource named XULA. The resource XULA can be either rented or can be bought. Many team members are in favor of buying the resource, whereas a few team members are in favor of renting. The buying cost for XULA is 10K (10,000). The resource rental for each month is 1K (1,000). The team has forecasted for the resource usage to last 4 months if everything goes well. In the worse scenario, the resource may be required for 15 months, but most likely, the resource usage will end within 10 months. What would be your advice to James and the team?

    A. Buy the resource XULA as the most likely period is forecasted to be 10 months

    B. Buy the resource XULA as the worst-case scenario for resource requirement is 18 months

    C. Rent the resource XULA as the optimistic scenario is only 4 months

    D. Rent the resource XULA as the expected duration falls below the buying cost of XULA.

24. Another resource WINPIN-X is required for the project. Some specific resources, namely architects, will need this resource to simulate and test the entire architecture and provide guidance to the project. As of now, it's not clear how many architects will be on board. This is a very crucial resource and needs to be bought as and when the architects join the team. The requirement may be far in the future, but you need to build the cost in the project cost forecast. Which procurement strategy would you suggest to the Project Manager, James?

   A. Float an RFI to get initial cost estimates for the maximum no of architects on the project.

   B. Float an RFI to get per unit cost estimates

   C. Float an RFP to get initial cost estimates for the maximum no of architects on the project.

   D. Float an RFP to get per unit cost estimates

25. James, while planning for the project METRO-D, saw one of the requirements which needed more detailing. The requirement was that after the construction of the project, some of the constructed corridors could be used for advertising. It is yet not clear as to how many and what portion can be outsourced and to whom. When you contacted the customer, the customer admitted that they have no clarity on the said requirement and they would need some time for a clear picture to emerge. James' organization is a world leader in the field of construction but has minimum knowledge in the advertising domain. What is your suggestion for James?

   A. Keep this package as a planning package as of now and deal with it later

   B. Mark this package as one of the threats to the project and discuss it with stakeholders

   C. Mark this package as an opportunity and discuss it with stakeholders

   D. Mark this package to be outsourced as a cost-plus contract

26. James' team created the procurement statement of work for the advertising work package. They also listed another document called terms of reference (TOR). What would you typically find in a TOR?

   A. Contract type to be used with the supplier

   B. The negotiated amount for the contract

   C. The work description of the work package

   D. Standards that contractor will fulfil as applicable

27. James and the team started working on the project deliverables. The team is busy executing the activities as per the project plan. One of the activities listed is to get initial estimates for the resource WINPIN-X. What would be the first step to initiate the procurement?

    A.   Proposal evaluations

    B.   Advertising

    C.   Independent estimates

    D.   Bidder conferences

28. Commonly used source selection methods include the following (Select 2):

    ☐   A. Sole source

    ☐   B. Per unit

    ☐   C. Qualifications only

    ☐   D. One source

29. Once the supplier for WINPIN-X is selected, James orders 3 licenses of WINPIN-X as per the list price submitted by the supplier for various types of licenses. The licenses are either user-based licenses or machine-based licenses. With user-based licenses, a user can use the license on any number of machines. With machine-based licenses, a machine will be installed with the software WINPIN-X, and any number of users can access the software. Which contact type is used by James to buy WIN-PIN-X?

    A.   Fixed-price

    B.   Cost plus

    C.   Time & material

    D.   Cost plus with rates

30. James is confused with the terms of inspection and audit. Please simplify:

    A.   Inspection is carried out for deliverables or a physical review of the work, whereas audits are performed on the processes

    B.   Audit is carried out for deliverables or a physical review of the work, whereas inspection is performed on the processes

4.6.2 ANSWERS: PROCESS | PROCUREMENT MANAGEMENT

Answer	Why
Answer 1 - A	If you have a fully developed SOW, then as a buyer, the better contract type is fixed price, as the risk of price escalation is boxed. Fixed-price contracts are safest for the buyer and help ensure that the SOW is developed clearly.
Answer 2 - C	This question asks you which contracting type is to be used in a different way. Let's look at the problem statement. You need specific resources for a small period of time. Now, does it qualify for total outsourcing as an FP contract? No, so answer A is out. Do you need to hire employees full-time? Not necessarily. Even on this project, you need specialized resources only for some time. So, choice B is also eliminated. Choice D, to ask the customer, may be a good option if you don't get people from the market, but the most suitable choice is C, where you can hire such resources as consultants on a time and material basis.
Answer 3 - B	Fixed Price with Economic Price Adjustment Contracts (FP-EPA) - This contract type is used whenever the seller's performance period spans a considerable period of years, as is desired with many long-term relationships. It is a fixed-price contract, but with a special provision allowing for predefined final adjustments to the contract price due to changed conditions, such as inflation changes or cost increases (or decreases) for specific commodities.
Answer 4 - B	Cost Plus Incentive Fee Contracts (CPIF): The seller is reimbursed for all allowable costs for performing the contract work and receives a predetermined incentive fee based upon achieving certain performance objectives as set forth in the contract.
Answer 5 - A	This is the BEST answer type of question. Let's analyze:
Answer 6 - B	Pre-bid meetings should be facilitated to respond to any queries raised by sellers. The idea is that all the sellers should get responses to all the questions, thus achieving no bias of information between sellers.

Answer 7 - A, C	Project delivery methods include but are not limited to Turnkey, Design-Build (DB), Design Bid Build (DBB), Design-Build Operate (DBO), Build Own Operate Transfer (BOOT).
Answer 8 - B	Incentives and awards may be used to align the objectives of buyer and seller. The correct answer is: TRUE
Answer 9 - B	The phrase terms of reference (TOR) is sometimes used when contracting for services. Similar to the procurement SOW, a TOR typically includes these elements: → specified requirements criteria, standards, and process adherence → Report formats and data to be submitted etc.
Answer 10 - A	This is a straightforward answer. The highest technical marks are given to Seller A, Seller A also the lowest-cost vendor.
Answer 11 - B	You get two keywords here: Specifications are not developed, i.e., SOW is an unclear and risky work package. Go with cost-plus contracting.
Answer 12 - D	This might take some time to sink in. You are a seller and not a Project Manager from the buyer organization. So, if you are a seller, the better contracts are cost-plus and time and material. So, choices A and B are eliminated. Between choices C and D, which one is better? With a cost-plus incentive fee, the seller shares the profits as well as losses per the pre-defined formula. In the case of D, you get a cost-plus award. Awards are based on your performance, but that's under your control (meaning your team's control), so the best contract type for the seller would be choice D—cost-plus award fee contracts.
Answer 13 - C	Typically, the buyer organization sets up a mechanism to settle disputes. A third-party team is formed at the buyer's discretion to manage and settle disputes.
Answer 14 - B	Check the keyword "rate list." Simple: it's a time and material procurement.
Answer 15 - D	Sole source procurement is used when only a specific seller is identified to have a unique capability and is the only provider for the required work. In such cases, only one supplier is asked to submit a proposal.

Answer 16 - D	RFI, RFQ, and RFP are all related to requesting information/quotes/proposals and are the first step while buying. Pre-bid meetings happen after RFP, RFI, or RFQ is advertised and hence is the odd one out.
Answer 17 - B	Typically, procurement strategy documents contain all the information on what type of contracts to be used. Check the PMBOK for more details.
Answer 18 - D	Control procurement deals with closing the procurements when the work is accomplished. Make or buy analysis is part of planning procurements and not a correct answer. Validate scope is acceptance testing by the customer and is not a correct answer.
Answer 19 - C	Mike is a buyer in this scenario. Since SOW is fully developed, which contract type would you select as a buyer? Bang on—fixed price. Choice D and B are eliminated. Now, between EPA or FP with incentive fee, which one is better? Incentives are based on seller performance; if the seller performs well, then you as a buyer give incentives. Bingo—FPIF is the best answer.
Answer 20 - A	The highest technical score is given to seller A, whom you will select even if the bid amount is higher. Why? Because the selection criteria are the highest technical score alone.
Answer 21 - A	Let's use the process of elimination. If you are a buyer and want to minimize outsourcing risks pertaining to cost, what will you select? Fixed price. Thus, choices C and D are eliminated. Between choice A and choice B, which one is better? Keeping a buffer in the project procurement phase may not help the project because the procurement could be an activity within any phase. The best choice is choice A where you will suggest selecting an FP contract to minimize the cost risk and monitor and control for schedule delays.

Answer 22 - B	Which document lists the contract type to be used for the project: Procurement strategy. When to buy and when the deliverable is due are listed in the project schedule. Choice B is the most correct option.
Answer 23 - D	This question requires you to remember the calculations for PERT and average distribution to calculate the expected duration. This is the calculation:
Answer 24 - B	This should be a rate contract. That's clear, right? Would you float an RFI or RFP? You are not intending to buy right now but want to buy in the future. In such cases, the buyer floats an RFI (Request for information) to get the cost estimates. The best answer is B: get per unit cost, using an RFI.
Answer 25 - C	Let's check each answer one by one: A. Keep this package as a planning package as of now and deal with it later: **This is not a good option as I need to know the risks of this package.** B. Mark this package as one of the threats to the project and discuss it with stakeholders: **It can be a good choice to select. Let's see if we get a better answe**r. C. Mark this package an opportunity for the project and discuss it with stakeholders: **Can this work package give you the opportunity to earn more money? Yes, sharing the opportunity may yield newer streams and better earnings on the project, a better choice than B.** D. Mark this package to be outsourced as a cost-plus contract: **This is not a good choice to select. Why do we mark anything for outsourcing? We check for risks, costs, and skillsets, to name a few of the reasons. Risk analysis along with make or buy should be performed before making any work package for outsourcing.** By checking all the answers, the best answer is C.
Answer 26 - D	The phrase terms of reference (TOR) is sometimes used when contracting for services. Similar to the procurement SOW, a TOR typically includes these elements:

→ specified requirements criteria, standards, and process adherence

→ Report formats and data to be submitted etc.

Answer 27 - B	To initiate the procurements, you advertise. Check the RECAP section to understand the flow of events for procurement.
Answer 28 - A, C	Per unit is contract type – T&M. One source is not a recognized term. The correct answer is Sole Source and Qualifications only. All the source selection criteria are given below for your reference:

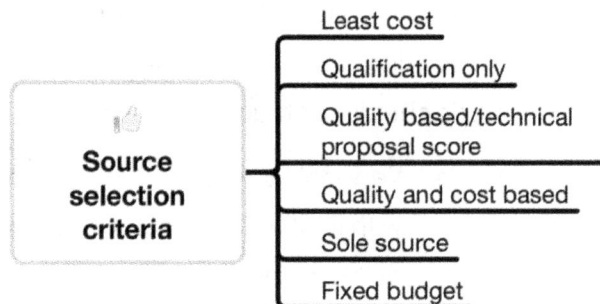

Least cost

Qualification only

Quality based/technical proposal score

Source selection criteria

Quality and cost based

Sole source

Fixed budget

Answer 29 - C	There is much theory in the scenario, and the question is only in the last line. **You will get such verbose questions in the PMP exam.** So, check the question asked first and see if you really need to read the full scenario. It's a dirty trick but works when you have less time. Using keywords will also help you to understand the scenario. What is the keyword in this question? 3 licenses (units). It is a time & material contract.
Answer 30 - A	Inspection is carried out for deliverables or a physical review of the work, whereas audits are performed on the processes.

15. ABOUT KAVITA SHARMA

Kavita Sharma
Significant Contributor
PMBOK- Sixth Edition

Kavita Sharma has two decades of project management experience in IT, Project Management, Program Management, Account Management, and Project and Leadership Coaching.

She worked with Microsoft, Tech Mahindra, Sapient, and Satyam in her career. While working as an end-to-end program manager, she managed multi-skilled virtual teams ranging from 30 - 90 members having widespread skill sets.

In the last few years (approx. 10), she has evolved as a great mentor to the PMP aspirants and conducts project management workshops. She authored many books, including the best seller:

Pass PMP in 21 Days - Study Guide.

You can see her name in the PMBOK as a significant contributor and CAPM (eLearning by PMI) reviewer.

Her focus is now shifting to mindfulness. We hope to see something new from her pretty soon.

YouTube: https://www.youtube.com/channel/UCLjfEAI-EmgzsDQnXiTth9g

Linkedin: https://www.linkedin.com/in/kavitasharmapmp

Official Website: https://KavitaSharma.net

THANK YOU

Hi, this is Kavita Sharma. Thanks for buying the book and staying with it till the end. I assume that you have gone through the book and stayed with it. And that is the reason you are reading this page.

A lot of effort has gone into producing this book.

I keep receiving feedback from people like you and ensure that the feedback is acted upon. That's the reason you see book updates.

The credit goes to all of you.

I hope that you found the book helpful. If there is any feedback do write to me. I will look forward to hearing from you. You can reach me at kavita.sh@gmail.com.

Thanks, and wishing you success.

Kavita Sharma

Author, Coach, and Thinker

DISCLAIMER

With this book, I have put in my best effort to bring you the right tools to pass the PMP examination. However, this should not be interpreted as a promise or guarantee of your success. Any positive or negative outcome is ultimately dependent on your competency, commitment, and the overall effort put into the PMP exam preparation.
You have the right tools with you. Use them and pass the PMP exam.